THE SOCIAL CAUSE DIET

Other books by Gail Perry Johnston

A RUMOR OF ANGELS:
QUOTATIONS FOR LIVING, DYING & LETTING GO,
Coauthored With Jill Perry Rabideau

THE WISH & THE WONDER:
WORDS OF WISDOM FOR EXPECTANT PARENTS

THE SOCIAL CAUSE DIET

Find A Service That Feeds Your Soul

GAIL PERRY JOHNSTON

Cupola
PRESS®

www.cupolapress.com

© 2008 by Gail Perry Johnston

Published in Lafayette, California by Cupola Press™

Library of Congress Control Number: 2008900588

ISBN-13: 978-0-9793345-2-8
ISBN-10: 0-9793345-2-7

Scripture, unless otherwise noted, taken from the HOLY BIBLE, NEW INTERNATIONAL VERSION®. Copyright © 1973, 1978, 1984 International Bible Society. Used by permission of Zondervan. All rights reserved.

Printed in the United States of America

Thank you, Lauren Holcomb, for your generous help editing these stories. You were exactly what I needed.

Thanks to confidants Dean and Sharon Ruddell and creative colleagues Colleen Marquez and Amy McRoberts.

My profuse thanks also goes to the contributors. The word "anthology" literally means "garland" or "bouquet of flowers"— an appropriate description of your stories that collectively and beautifully demonstrate the Social Cause Diet.

Table of Contents

5   **INTRODUCTION**

9   **PART ONE:** *Reflections*

11 A Bigger World

15 A Longer View

19 In the Moment

21 Fulfilling Friends

25 Addicted to Entertainment

29 Not the Full Story

31 Random Acts of Kindness

35 In Praise of Parent Volunteers

39 The Complexities of Guilt

45 Believable

49 2,000 Calories A Day

53 **PART TWO:** *Stories of Satisfying Service*

55 Yancey   *Shaun Groves*

57 I Call it Therapy   *Janet Huckabee*

59 Horse Sense and Weight Loss   *Carolyn Escorico*

63 A Fashionable Service   *Triston McLaughlin*

67 Two Thumbs Up   *Cody Fisher*

69 My First Avon Breast Cancer Walk   *Michelle Bermas*

73   Writing for the Cure   *Elizabeth Fishel*

79   Mbali   *Dr. Maithri Goonetilleke*

81   Before Their Time   *Michael Whitman*

85   No Lunch for Lent   *Sean Blomquist*

87   In Concert with my Dad   *Elizabeth Stookey Sunde*

91   Twelve Minute Cab Ride   *Nipun Mehta*

95   Legislative Birdwatchers   *Joan Reinhardt Reiss*

99   Kids Helping Kids   *Laura Page*

103   Life at the Kettle   *Rev. Beth Ernest*

109   Kenny   *Chris Malcomb*

119   When Consumerism Calls   *Michele Sbrana*

123   The Open Door   *Lynn Turner*

127   Voluntary Eating   *Lisa Ota*

131   Loving the Main   *Bill Hayes*

133   Accidental Family   *Jessica Brophy*

139   How to be a Kick-Butt Volunteer   *Shyla Batliwalla*

143   Inside Addition   *Jes Steinberg*

147   A Light Change   *Avery Hairston*

149   Malcolm—In Memoriam   *Larry Nilson*

153   SERVE   *Colleen D.C. Marquez*

155   The Spirit of a Child   *Karen Henrich*

157   Confessions from the Peace Corps   *Nikki Maxwell*

161   A Two Hour Walk with Grandma Bette   *Bette Simons*

163   Pack Pencils   *Patricia Costello*

165   Writing Through the Darkness   *Elizabeth Maynard Schaefer*

169 No Staying Quiet *Sandra Kay*

173 The Threshold Choir *Kate Munger*

175 Forgiven *Kellie Pauley*

177 Vision *Dr. Maithri Goonetilleke*

179 Driving by the Accident *Justin McRoberts*

181 All Children Have Good Cents *Dagmar Serota*

183 Meant for this Moment *Gina Garcia*

185 Helping Those Without Speech *Patricia Brown*

189 Angels with Four Paws *Christine Gonyea*

193 Sacred Conference Calls *Michael Gingerich*

197 Fried Turkey and Boiled Crawfish *Matthew Calkins*

199 A Gentle People's Last Hope *Eric P. Nichols*

203 Street Star *Brenda K. Blakely*

207 Our Boy *Shannon Lowe*

209 Music of a Stolen Symphony *Nipun Mehta*

213 **PART THREE:** *Final Reflections & Resources*

215 How Much Do I Give?

219 A Calling and a Caution

223 When Service Goes Awry

227 The Whole Process

231 Serving with Your Personality Type *Jody Bagno*

232 The Social Cause Diet Personality Test *Jody Bagno*

239 Matching Services

242 Index of Organizations and Contributors

INTRODUCTION

Volunteering and health appear to be tied together. Evidence suggests that a regimen of helping others may be as important to our physical well-being as regular exercise and proper nutrition. Over the past two decades, a growing body of research has shown that a pattern of giving may actually increase one's life span and that those who volunteer have lower mortality rates, greater functional ability and lower rates of depression than those who do not volunteer.*

The sacrificial giving of one's time and talents is no longer just reserved for so-called saints. We now know that it is an important part of maintaining optimal health for us all. Medically speaking, an infection-fighting antibody apparently kicks in when a person is engaged in serving others. But there's more to it than that. There are mysterious, spiritual blessings that can't be seen or measured but that surely enhance our well-being and quality of life. Thus, this book proposes that we are all candidates for the *Social Cause Diet*. This diet is not exactly easy, but it is unabashedly rich and satisfying. Moreover, it is the healthiest diet around, with benefits for both you and society at large.

I have volunteered for one organization or another since my early teens, so I have many wonderful stories of service under my belt. These are stories of connecting with small children to teens to aging adults while learning, laughing, loving, and feeding my soul along the way.

Unfortunately, I have even more experience with another kind of diet—although these stories aren't as pleasant. At age seven, I began to obsess about what I should eat and not eat. I remember that fateful day when I sat on the curb next to the tiniest girl in second grade and compared, of all things, our knee bones. Her knees were half the size of mine, so I concluded I was fat. She probably grew up with osteoporosis. And I grew up with an intense eating disorder.

For years I avoided food like it was the enemy, but with every denial of a decent meal, I only craved it more. After a full day of magnificent self-control, I would break down and eat whatever I could find. On top of that, I would succumb to overeating when I didn't know where else to go with my emotional needs or anxieties, all the while repeating to myself that tiresome mantra that I would do better the next day.

Today, I am thrilled to be free from all that drama. A few of my reflections in Part One of *The Social Cause Diet* disclose the turning points in my healing, one being the epiphany that while there was a big world out there, mine was getting smaller and shallower as I focused more and more of my energies on my diet. In other words, I realized I was becoming increasingly self-absorbed and no longer wanted to continue on that path.

Perhaps the weight issues of our country aren't due so much to eating as they are to a poor focus. Rather than directing our attention to grander pursuits, we simply buy another diet book. More than 430 diet books were published in the United States last year, yet obesity is at an all-time high and eating disorders are on the rise. Typically, diet books have one major flaw: they make the dieter the focal point, endorsing the ideology that "it's all about me." But true well-being—philosophers, theologians and sociologists all agree—is achieved when we feel connected to something *beyond* ourselves. I don't think we need another new program for losing weight, but we do need a plan for losing a little of *ourselves*. We could use some guidance for getting the attention off of our obsessions and our appetites and onto things that are beyond our personal existence.

Part Two of this book consists of firsthand accounts by people who, knowingly or unknowingly, are on the Social Cause Diet. They have incorporated acts of service into their lifestyle and have discovered that it really is more blessed to give than to receive. Some volunteers, but not all, find serving to be an extension of their faith. Their stories, as well as some of my writings, reflect that. Some of the stories have been included not because of their great plot, but because of the beautiful attitude of the contributor. Regardless, the overriding message is that volunteering brings life-enhancing rewards that far exceed the efforts we put into it.

There are limitless varieties of the Social Cause Diet. It is easier than ever to find one that works for you. The number of nonprofit organizations is expanding, fueled in part by baby boomers—now older and wealthier—who are turning to philanthropic ventures. There are well-known organizations such as the Red Cross, but there are also lesser-known ones that tackle an incredible array of needs. From cleaning up after an oil spill, to caring for orphans in Liberia, to volunteering at a museum—there are countless opportunities.

This book provides no pecking order to the available causes to serve, because there shouldn't be any. Treating an infant with AIDS may, on the surface, seem more important than helping out at the local library, but who's to say? The case can be made that the library volunteer plays a critical role in helping develop the love of learning in a young person who may, one day, find a cure for AIDS. Besides, we are all gifted in different ways. We each have our own set of talents and interests, and the loveliest blessings will come when we discover where we are best suited.

The range of services represented in Part Two will help you find causes that appeal to you or organizations that support the causes you already know are important to you. In addition, Part Three offers a simple personality test that will indicate where you will be most comfortable and productive as a participant.

I wish you the best as you try the Social Cause Diet. There is no reason to be skeptical of it. It has been tried and tested. It is not a passing fad. In all honesty, it will cost you something—your time, energy and maybe money. It may be difficult and uncomfortable. Yet the benefits are well worth it. The following stories testify to that fact. And unlike those diets that leave you hungry, this one will fill you up.

* For the full report, "The Health Benefits of Volunteering: A Review of Recent Research" and other reports on volunteering, visit www.nationalservice.org.

PART ONE

Reflections

*"He who refreshes others
will himself be refreshed."*

PROVERBS 11:25

Maturity begins to grow when you can
sense your concern for others outweighing
your concern for yourself.

JOHN MACNAUGHTON

A Bigger World

I had an eating disorder long before eating disorders became a national concern. One college day I was in serious anguish over my consumption of a small package of cheese crackers and the money I wasted on it (only 25 cents at the time!). I had blown my diet again. I spent money on empty calories. I am such a loser. As I fussed, my annoyed roommate looked at me sternly and said with disgust in her voice, "Gail, the world is bigger than your 25 cents and bag of crackers." Wow. I wonder if Susie knew how profound she was being and how right she was. I wonder if she noticed that, right there in front of her, I was having an epiphany. Susie's simple statement blew through my brain and caused me to realize that my obsession with what I ate and didn't eat was making my world very small. All of a sudden, it was so clear to me that my eating disorder was robbing me of precious time and energy that could be spent in so many other constructive ways.

First of all, my poor eating habits were affecting my health, limiting my physical energy and abilities. But moreover, the cyclical treadmill I was on—dieting, then overeating, then getting sick, then feeling guilty—preoccupied my mind to such a degree that there was little space left to think of anything else.

It's ironic that my very first best friend, Stacy, grew up to become a specialist on eating disorders. As adults, we lived on opposite sides of the country and lost touch with each other, so I had no idea that I could have accessed her expertise when I needed it. Now back in touch, I shared with her the concept for the Social Cause Diet— the concept that the best diet around is one that consists of healthy servings of service to others. She loved it and gave me her take on it. She was hesitant at first, because she didn't want to seem crass, but then she said, "There's a time and place for helping my clients figure out why they need things to be all about them. And then there's a time to get on with it."

I'd like to say that I was able to "get on with it" after my encounter with Susie, but I needed professional help. The college therapist didn't do much for me, but when I moved to New York City, I called a psychiatrist who was considered the leading expert in eating disorders. Of course, she was all booked up, so I resorted to begging for an appointment. It is not my style to beg anyone for anything, but I had a sense that if I could just have a brief time with her, I could get a jumpstart on my problem. She finally agreed to meet me for twenty minutes. Sparing you the details of that quick session, suffice it to say that it met my expectations wonderfully and pointed me in the right direction for productive time with subsequent therapists.

It took about three years of hard work to learn what I needed to learn to get over my eating disorder. This book would not have been possible if I didn't have that intense phase of focusing on myself so I could go *beyond* myself. In the reflections I've written for this book, there is nothing I share lightly—everything I offer is the result of my earnest pursuit for healing and the ensuing freedom.

If you are in a place where you have an all-consuming problem and you need to figure out why something has gotten such a grip on you, get help. The Social Cause Diet is surely a solution, but it is not claiming to be the only answer if you are a candidate for professional attention or a group like AA or OA (just some of the "Anonymous" organizations that are working wonders for people of all ages and backgrounds). Resources abound, so you can surely find adequate help if you stick your neck out. Please don't play games by making *one* appearance at *one* meeting and announcing that it doesn't work for you. You've got to give people a chance. If a group truly isn't your style, look for another. If a therapist doesn't impress you, ask for references for someone else. You may also want to investigate the new medications that are being developed and tested for addictive persons.*

On the other hand, if you are ready to get over yourself and get on with it, it's time for the Social Cause Diet. This diet is about adapting a lifestyle that is bigger and better than you ever imagined. It's about breaking the boundaries of your own existence and discovering you have the capacity for much more than yourself. It's about growing up and becoming mature as described by John MacNaughton at the start of this reflection.

Contrary to what our youth may be learning, "mature" doesn't just mean a rating on a violent video game or a movie with explicit sex. Maturity, in the proper sense of the word, means being aware of what is going on within your own heart, mind and soul and then taking the next step of being attentive to those around you; it means being able to make willful decisions that benefit your own health and wellbeing and then advancing to the point of making decisions for the benefit of others, at times sacrificially.

None of us will ever be perfectly mature, but we can hope to always be moving closer to the mark. Being intentional about serving others is key for everyone. Those who are young and inexperienced; those who are ambitious and overworked; those who are middle-aged and questioning; those who are elderly and aging—all can be continually experiencing the inner expansion that comes from realizing it's not "all about me." There's so much more.

Gary Haugen, inspiring speaker and author of *Good News About Injustice,* likes to say, "May God save us from triviality." He metaphorically challenges us to use our strength for more than just opening that stubborn jar of jelly in the kitchen. We can do greater things than that. There is a big world beyond our kitchen. As we grow in awareness of others and occasionally show beautiful signs of maturity by putting their needs before our own, we become bigger ourselves.

---

*Read about new medications in "What Addicts Need" by Jeneen Interlandi, *Newsweek, March 3, 2008.*

Is it possible to be full and still hungry
at the same time?

LUKE JOHNSTON, *13-year-old*

We must ask ourselves, "How long does it last?
How deep does it go?"

DEAN HONNETTE, *on evaluating our priorities*

A Longer View

My mother used to be a high school librarian and absorbs information continuously. She frequently calls to tell me about the results of a recent survey. During one phone conversation, she reported, "The study revealed that people crave *food* more than sex." Ha! Maybe it's not obvious to others, but people crave food so much because we need it to live. While sex is necessary for the continuation of our kind, we actually won't experience a long and painful death from going without it.

The necessity of eating for survival is what makes our issues with food so hard to resolve. We have to repeatedly submit to the very thing that causes us to stumble. If we tend to turn to food obsessively like an alcoholic turns to drink, we are in a real fix. We can't go cold-turkey. We'll never be able to say, "I'm a recovering overeater and I haven't had a bite in six months." We have to take a different approach.

Now that I'm twenty years past my eating disorder, I look back with appreciation that I couldn't find an easy solution for my problem. I was living in New York City during the peak of my dysfunction, and food was everywhere—bagels on every corner, food carts wheeled through the office and restaurants open 24 hours a day. I had a real challenge. Fortunately, therapists were multiplying like bunnies in the '80s, and I found a competent one. I entered into a necessary phase of introspection and asked, "Why, oh, why can't I stop eating?"

I discovered that eating is not just a physical experience. There are emotional and spiritual things mixed up in it. Whether we are dining with our families at the kitchen table, sharing a special meal for two in an intimate restaurant, or attending a pig-picking party in the South, most eating events have something more going on than the mere consumption of food.

In America we love food. We are well-nourished by it. Yet, we want it to do even more for us. We want it to meet our emotional and spiritual needs. And, to some degree, it does! The wonderful scene in the Pixar film "Ratatouille" shows the transformation that occurs when a damaged old man tastes a delicious ratatouille that takes him back to the loving environment of his childhood kitchen. Food can do that. But day after day, meal after meal, we are asking too much if we are expecting delectables to satisfy us, reward us, calm our anxieties, or pacify our troubled minds.

Tonight after dinner, my thirteen-year-old son asked me this question: "Is it possible to be full and still hungry at the same time?" Well, yes, I was tempted to say. If you turn to food to fill the empty places in your heart and soul, you will be forever hungry. But I restrained myself because in his case, as I told him, he had just defined what it means to be a growing teenager. For the rest of us, however, if we are still thinking of food and hungering for more when we should be content, we have some problem-solving to do.

For those of you not stuck in the preoccupation of your food intake, please stay with me. Food is not the only enticement that satisfies us nicely up to a point, but ultimately gets us in trouble if we expect it to meet needs it was not designed to meet. Your particular appetites may subject you to a dependence on entertainment, alcohol, accumulation of wealth, or any number of things. Whatever the case may be, it's wise to ask ourselves occasionally, "Do the things I pursue meet my inner needs? What are their spiritual rewards? Are the benefits lasting, or do they dissolve as fast as sugar on the tongue?"

Jonathan Edwards, a theologian and the third president of Princeton University, wrote this in his diary:

> Frequently in my Pursuits of whatever Kind,
> let this come into my Mind;
> "How much shall I value this on my Death Bed?"

Not many of us keep diaries today, much less compose rhymes to evaluate the importance of our pursuits, but we would be significantly better off in our world today and in our private lives if we regained a longer view. You see, if we look ahead and contemplate the value of a thing or experience in light of the future, we can better assess its present value. For example, we may really, really want a chocolate chip cookie that is tempting us; but in ten years, will we remember it? It's highly unlikely that we will, so it's safe to say that consuming the cookie isn't something we have to do. Once we put the cookie in its proper place in the grand scheme of things, it's not as powerful—and *we* have become more so! With our new perspective on the cookie, we discover we have the ability to pass on it, if that's what we determine would be best.

Our culture isn't keen on the long view. Rather, we prefer instant gratification and the here and now. It's fascinating, really, how we can get instant messages and instant mashed potatoes. But the downside of our rapid-fire technology is that we can develop a very short view and an unhealthy way of assessing things. Our modus operandi becomes "the faster, the better" or "get it while the getting's good."

I am still puzzled by certain encounters I had while living in Greenville, North Carolina. There I met true Southerners who didn't believe in the faster-is-better rule. They would take the long way home "just because" and look at me for way too many minutes before saying anything. It drove me crazy. I was too hyper for that town, and I probably still am. But I have come to understand, particularly now as a parent, that there is something to be said for *deferred* gratification—having to wait for something. We are stretched from Point A (when we decide we want something) to Point B (when we get it). Through this stretching we gain patience and perspective. Our view is lengthened. It is not just the here and now that is important, but tomorrow and the next day and the day after that.

We are doing our children a favor when we say, "No, you can't have that right now. Instead, you have to save your allowance for four months, and then you can buy it *yourself.*" Sure there will be fussing, but then the child will settle down and start to imagine four months ahead, developing a longer view. The *need* for instant gratification will be proven false, especially as the child experiences the reward, sweetened by anticipation, when the wait is over.

Incorporating the Social Cause Diet into our lives will help us develop a longer view, which in turn will help us play the waiting game, which, whether we resist it or not, is a reality of life. This step up in maturity is a natural result of serving. We often don't even realize it's happening. Serving others tends to cause things to shift around in our psyche so that matters of greater long-term importance and of deeper value start to rise to the top. Teaching a child to read, cleaning up after an oil spill, holding the hand of a dying person, fundraising for a good cause—all of these experiences impact our understanding of what truly matters. If we stick with the Social Cause Diet and continue to give of ourselves to others, we will eventually notice that we are not so subject to the enticements that used to entangle us, and we are not so upset when we don't "get it while it's hot." The story you'll read on page 119 exemplifies this. *When Consumerism Calls* tells how one lady's commitment to a cause gave her self-control she previously didn't have—just one of the reasons the Social Cause Diet is so healthy.

In the Moment

Having a long view and living in the moment are not mutually exclusive. They complement each other. Before you can assess the long-term value of something, you have to first be aware of what is going on around you and within you at that point in time. A turning point in my life came in the middle of a movie when I was 19 years old. I can't remember what the movie was because the point is, I wasn't really watching it. Although there in person, my mind was elsewhere. I was probably scrutinizing my diet again or worrying about schoolwork. After an hour of this, I recognized how pitiful it was to go to a movie to escape and not be able to succeed at it. I decided right then and there that I would start being mentally present wherever I was.

For the most part, I really was more in the moment after that. What relief! I had far less anxiety in my life because I was determined to not let my worries contaminate present engagements. Incidentally, this change was a step toward the healing of my eating disorder. Being anxious all day was a setup for overeating at night. Hours of mental stress without relief depleted my power of resistance by evening. But I discovered that if I put worry aside to attentively listen to a friend's story, for example, or truly relax when I took a coffee break, I was more peaceful at the end of the day, and I didn't turn to food to unwind. Stressing does not result in anything good.

Serving, on the other hand, does. When you serve, you are hard-pressed not to be in the moment. Before you is a house that has been destroyed by a flood or victims of a devastating disease. Or maybe it's a dog that needs a home or a community garden that needs pruning. Whatever it is, you've got a job to do or a cause to support. You get into it and you put yourself and your worries aside. This is healthy. This is stress-relieving. This is the Social Cause Diet.

Your face satisfies me
Like a sound summer sleeping
Like a gentle weeping
Like a pink bed with three pillows
Like a long lawn with low willows
Like a warm cat on my feet
Like a daydream treat

GAIL JOHNSTON

Who can live without friends?! None of us, though we
sometimes pretend otherwise for reasonable, yet ultimately
self-defeating, reasons. God said of Adam, even as they
strolled the garden together: "It is not good for the man
to be alone." We are designed for relationship, for human
companionship, for healthy and mutually-fulfilling intimacy.

DOUG STEVENS

Interdependence is and ought to be as much the ideal
of man as self-sufficiency. Man is a social being. Without
interrelation with society he cannot realize his oneness
with the universe or suppress his egotism.

MAHATMA GANDHI

Fulfilling Friends

Have you ever noticed there are some friends who fill you up and some who leave you drained? With some friends, no matter what you do together, you are left with a certain contentment. With others, you leave feeling the opposite.

I bike ride with Annette for two hard hours once or twice a month. We often ride side by side on back roads, pushing through twenty miles of hills while circling the beautiful Briones Park in the East Bay. We pass vineyards, horses, cows, goats, and even a pair of ewes.

Annette is an exuberant storyteller. She tells me about the challenges in her life. Whether or not they are mundane, they are always interesting because she shares with expression and with her honest emotions. More importantly, Annette is a great listener. When I tell her what's going on in my life, she listens attentively, saying, "Oh, no!" at all the right times. Inevitably, I share something of a spiritual nature, and whether or not she adheres to my beliefs, she always listens like a good friend and affirms me. There is freedom of all sorts when we bike: the freedom of moving fast and leaving our worries behind and the freedom to express ourselves without fear of judgment. When the ride is over, my legs are wobbly and my neck hurts, but my soul is happy.

Conversely, there are friends who leave me with feelings of emptiness. Maybe they are uncaring or just plain shallow. Maybe they are too self-absorbed to have a give-and-take conversation. Or maybe it's me! Maybe my insecurities and shyness are keeping me from building a real relationship with these people.

In our efforts to find friends who fill us up, we have to look at ourselves first. One of the best how-to books of all time is Dale Carnegie's *How to Win Friends & Influence People*. This book should be required reading in high school—better yet, in sixth grade. The concepts are simple but often missed. If you haven't read it yet, it's not too late. If you haven't read it in ages, you may want to check it out it again. After eighteen years of marriage, I determined that my husband needed to read this book and begged him to buy a copy. Being the smart man that he is, he went out and bought two copies—one for both of us. Now approaching our twentieth anniversary, I can testify that this book helped my husband and me finally begin treating each other as best friends. We are still ridiculously imperfect in our communication skills, but we are getting there. We have made huge steps forward in our ability to listen to each other and to show the kind of care and attention that nourishes the soul.

Intimacy, according to minds much more studied than mine, is a matter of tuning in to someone else's reality with the risk of being changed by the experience. It is *not* a matter of extending your self-absorption to include someone else.[1] The Social Cause Diet is a catalyst for intimacy and true friendship because this diet requires that you leave your self-absorption behind and focus on others. By so doing, you will develop real connections with the people you serve or with those who serve alongside you. You will taste and see how good an unselfish, caring relationship can be, whether it's one that lasts just for the duration of the service or one that lasts a lifetime. And you will like it. The next thing you know, you will apply what you have learned to your relationships at work, home, and elsewhere, achieving more fulfillment in every realm.

C.S. Lewis, my favorite writer, who had in equal measure great intelligence and boundless imagination, wrote an insightful book called *The Great Divorce*. Lewis was not speaking of divorce between two people, but of the chasm between heaven and hell. His description of hell is one I'll never forget. He pictured it as a grey town where people quarreled with their neighbors and then moved farther and farther away from each other until there was no community at all and hardly even a sighting of another person. When I get disappointed with a neighbor or friend and I'm tempted to write him or her off, I think of hell being a place where everyone ends up alone because it's easier than learning how to get along. Hell, in Lewis' analogy, is a complete disconnectedness from others. It is loneliness night and day without relief.

As volunteerism promotes health, loneliness seems to diminish it. One study revealed that lonely people have blood pressure readings that are as much as thirty points higher than non-lonely people.[2] Some researchers claim that the magnitude of health risk associated with social isolation is comparable to that of cigarette smoking.[3]

Loneliness is an emotion that tells us it's time to bring people into our lives. Some people boast about being independent and self-reliant, but if they are so, they are probably somewhat lonely. A healthier, happier soul seeks to be *interdependent*. In the Social Cause Diet, as you selflessly meet the needs of others, some of your own needs are met, such as your need for companionship, appreciation, and a sense of purpose. Be sure to read *Sacred Conference Calls* for a beautiful story of interdependence. While it is extremely unkind to *use* each other, it is right and wise to realize that we are mutually *useful* to each other. We all have something to give to and gain from those around us.

This usefulness isn't a measurable give-and-take thing, by the way. I give hours of emotional support to a friend, for example, and then she comes through for me in fantastic, unexpected ways. But even if she didn't surprise me by taking care of my kids in an emergency or by teaching me how to make brussel sprouts that taste amazing, I still always feel blessed after helping her. It's a mystery, really—a very fulfilling one.

1. Stephanie Dowrick, *Intimacy and Solitude*, W.W. Norton & Company, 1991.
2. Lori Rackl, *Being lonely hazardous to your heart*, Chicago Sun-Times, March 28, 2006. The article cites findings by a team of researchers from The University of Chicago with lead researcher, Louise Hawkley.
3. James S. House, PH.D., *Social Isolation Kills, But How and Why?* Psychosomatic Medicine, 2001; 63.

Increasing the intensity of stimulation in our lives can actually spoil our capacity for enjoyment.

Tolerating less stimulation in our lives can actually increase our pleasure.

MARK CHAMBERLAIN, PH.D., *Wanting More: Challenge of Enjoyment in the Age of Addiction*

The ability to simplify means to eliminate the unnecessary so that the necessary may speak.

HANS HOFMANN

Addicted to Entertainment

My pastor claims we are all addicted to entertainment. Admittedly, my eye begins to twitch if it has been a few months since I've rented a movie. Statistics say Americans watch a ghastly amount of TV per week. It's best not to tell you the actual hours so you don't think you're better than the next guy. In my opinion, anything more than two hours a week spent in front of the tube is too much. That said, my eleven-year-old daughter recently inducted me into the fan pool of "American Idol." This is a heavy commitment. To be honest, I am enjoying the performances, but I often speculate how much more talented Americans would be if we all worked on our own musical skills instead of watching the Idols for hours on end.

Entertainment is any diversion that offers amusement and stimulation. For some, shopping is entertainment. Shopping distracts us from the matters of the day and is visually stimulating. An acquaintance once told me that after a distressing argument with her husband, she went to Costco and bought $600 worth of goods, most of which were completely frivolous. That was the most fun she had all week! But the consequences weren't so desirable: a big bill to pay and lots of stuff to pile on top of other stuff she bought the last time she needed an escape. Eating can be entertainment, too. We've all been to parties where the main event is the meal. Eating is enjoyable pretty much anywhere—in the presence of fine company or alone in our kitchen with a dreamy bowl of ice cream.

There are many forms of entertainment, but they all share certain benefits that keep us coming back for more. Temporary relief from stress is the biggest one. The pleasurable activity takes our mind off ourselves and our problems. Next in line would be the connections we make with others who are sharing in the fun. Whether we are on a boat with our buddies or in bed with our spouse, we are making connections that expand and enhance our life.

Wow, you may be thinking—the benefits of entertainment sound a lot like those of social service! Maybe we should all go on the Entertainment Diet! But there is a problem with such a diet, and it's called *addiction*. In his book, *Wanting More,* Dr. Mark Chamberlain claims that we are presently in "the age of addiction." If we are not careful, our entertaining activity of choice can become an addiction such that we want more and more of it and start to believe that we *need* it to go on. And that may even be true! Our bodies get attached to our habits, and even if we are not predisposed to addiction, none of us are immune to the possibility of getting hooked. Call it human nature, lack of self-control, or a disease—we all tend to want too much of a good thing.

This is where the Social Cause Diet is so helpful. Practically speaking, if we introduce a few hours of service into our week, we will have less time to overdose on entertainment. In addition, when we serve others, we often become acutely aware of how lucky we are. Afterwards, we don't feel quite so in need of that shopping spree or trip to Cold Stone Creamery. In other words, the Social Cause Diet is a wonderful way to keep our appetites and addictive personalities in check. Lastly, as the quotes at the beginning of this reflection communicate, having less entertainment in our lives can actually increase the pleasure we obtain from each enjoyable event.

The paradox that less is more is easily demonstrated with toddlers. Put a kid in a room that is packed with toys, and he or she will soon get overwhelmed and unengaged. But put the little person in a room with a reasonable number of playthings, and the child brightens, picks up a toy, and maintains interest in it for a fair amount of time.

This principle holds true for kids as they get older. It never ceases to amaze me how fellow parents allow and even orchestrate constant stimulus for their kids, popping in one movie after another on long drives or planning all-day birthday parties that turn into all-night sleepovers. Where is the breathing room for the brain? Where is the chance to reflect on what just happened and anticipate what's next? My old-fashioned mother insisted that all four of her children rest on their individual beds for at least thirty minutes at some time each day. It wasn't for sleeping but for rest. And it certainly wasn't for text messaging because that wasn't invented yet! It was an enforced practice until we were tweens, and then we more or less kept it up on our own accord. For me, it became my journal writing time. Too bad we are grownups now and there is no one to regulate our playthings and activities. We have to parent ourselves. We have to learn how to enjoy things fully and revel in them, but also to pace ourselves and refrain from going for more, more, more.

There is another reason to swap some pleasure-seeking time for time spent in service. So far, I have yet to mention the impact volunteers have on our communities because that goes without saying. Cities with high volunteer rates have lower crime, higher employment, better education, and a better quality of life, and they continue to improve as volunteer rates increase.* Just think what a better world we would have if everyone decided to replace one or two TV shows a week with something like tutoring a child or delivering a meal to the elderly.

Entertainment isn't bad in and of itself, but if we are filling every free minute with it, if we are more or less addicted to it, then it's time to go on the Social Cause Diet.

*Volunteering in America: 2007 City Trends and Rankings, www.nationalservice.org.

How far you go in life depends on your being tender with the young, compassionate with the aged, sympathetic with the striving and tolerant of the weak and strong. Because someday in life you will have been all of these.

GEORGE WASHINGTON CARVER

Nothing that we despise in the other man is entirely absent from ourselves. We must learn to regard people less in the light of what they do or don't do, and more in light of what they suffer.

DIETRICH BONHOEFFER

To feed men and not to love them is to treat them as if they were barnyard cattle. To love them and not to respect them is to treat them as if they were household pets.

MENCIUS

Not the Full Story

It's so easy to serve if you live in a big city. In my four years in Manhattan, I occasionally volunteered to stay overnight in various homeless shelters that were within walking distance of my apartment. My duties involved greeting the homeless as they arrived and helping them choose their beds and put on the sheets. I also put out fresh bread, donated by another volunteer, and offered everyone a spread of peanut butter from a humongous jar of Jiffy. It wasn't a tough job, but I am rich with memories of those nights.

My favorite shelter was housed in the basement of an old church. It was cold and damp, and mice scurried about. But it had beautiful architectural features and a wonderful sense of history with low arches and picturesque tiles in curious places. This particular shelter was for the exceptional homeless person. I was told that only those who had proven clear of any drug or alcohol addictions were welcome. Only twelve people were accepted on any given night. With such a small, decent crowd, we were all able to visit around a large, solid wood table that had the markings of a hundred years. The conversation was light, but every now and then, something deep would be shared. One evening a man told us his story. "I used to have a family and a good paying job," he said. "But then I had a car accident, and everyone in my family died except for me. I couldn't do anything after that."

Because of this man's story, which still moves me today, I am determined never to judge a homeless person—or anyone in need, for that matter. When serving, there is no place for judgment. Later, when it comes time to vote on a particular bill, we can apply our analytical brains and determine what might be right or wrong for society. But when we are in the field, it's best to put all of that aside and just try to meet the needs before us, knowing perfectly well that we don't know the full story.

An area where there tends to be a great deal of judgment is that of the mom on welfare who gets pregnant yet again. What's her problem?! But even here, we don't know the full story. Maybe the mom just wants more money from the government, but maybe not. I know of a person I'll call Janet. Janet was raised by a woman who did not believe evil existed. "Evil is just a matter of wrong thinking," her mom would tell her. When Janet was raped as a young teen, her mother did not provide an ounce of comfort and even denied the reality of it. With no recognition of the crime from her own mother, Janet never spoke of the incident again and could not find healing from it. She ended up with little self-worth. From then on, Janet let herself be taken advantage of by one man after another. She eventually lived on welfare with four kids by different and distant fathers. I do not approve of Janet's choices, but knowing about the hurt she experienced as a teen and the lack of adult help through it, I feel compassion for her. I bring her story to mind when I'm tempted to judge another.

I love Carver's words at the beginning of this reflection. When we experience life's hardships, we often grow in leaps and bounds in empathy and maturity. But wouldn't it be wonderful if we possessed compassion for the needy even if we haven't been in their shoes, even if we can't relate one bit to their weakness? Not knowing their full story, not needing to know their full story, we extend ourselves, without passing judgment, but with gratefulness that we are in a position to help.

Random Acts of Kindness

One of the purposes of this book is to inspire volunteerism within established organizations. That said, a person can surely lead a life of service without being connected to any group. All people, no matter how busy they are or what phase of life they are in, can choose to keep themselves primed for random acts of service. This variety of the Social Cause Diet isn't necessarily the easiest, but it is usually convenient and can be hugely rewarding and impactful.

I went to college in North Carolina where many of my schoolmates struggled financially. A bowl of popcorn seasoned with parmesan cheese from the pizza parlor or sugar from the coffee shop constituted an affordable dinner for some. But every now and then, I would hear about people being blessed with mysterious bags of groceries left on their doorsteps. No one ever found out how many people were behind this recurring good deed. There was never a note or explanation—just welcome bags of recently purchased food staples for random starving students.

I was not one of the recipients of this example of a random act of kindness, but I was nonetheless impacted by it. Everyone was! Honorable actions lift us all up a bit higher.

One day I was telling my kids about the heroic deeds of their great-great-grandfather, who was a missionary in Siam. Just then, my father-in-law, Grandpa George, knocked on the door. George would be the first to say that he was no missionary. His business was construction, and his service was providing for his family. But I had a hunch that he probably had a few awesome stories to his name. So I asked him, "Do you have any hero stories to tell your grandkids?" Without missing a beat, George explained that, not too long ago, he saw a car on fire by the side of the road. He pulled over and was surprised to see a stunned lady still in the driver's seat. Discovering that the door was jammed, he tugged her out of the broken window. This was no small feat, he explained, because she was a *big* woman! Right after he got her safely into the passenger seat of his own car, her car exploded.

"Wow," I said. "You saved her life. What did she say?"

"Nothing," George explained. "She was in shock."

George is not a big talker, so I'm sure this life-saving account would have gone untold if I hadn't asked him that question. I'm so glad I did. Now his random act of kindness not only saved a life, but it also served to inspire me, the grandkids, and maybe even you! If you ever need a conversation starter at a party or family reunion, ask who has a hero story to tell. There may be more honorable people in your midst than you ever realized.

Maybe you can't imagine yourself pulling big ladies through car windows or anonymously leaving groceries on a doorstep. Well, let me suggest that everyone and anyone, without a doubt and without any inconvenience, can incorporate into their lives the easiest act of kindness around: the act of giving a compliment. Granted, some people feel self-conscious about giving compliments. In this case, my simple instruction is to *get over it*. Throw a compliment out there and see the good that it does and then it'll be easier the next time.

Excuse me for being so elementary, but in case it's not obvious, the key people to compliment are listed below:

- Your spouse or significant other
- Your kids
- Your parents and other relatives
- People you work for and people who work for you
- Coworkers and colleagues
- Mentors, teachers, counselors, etc.
- Your friends
- Your kids' friends
- Strangers/neighbors

That pretty much covers it. Those toward the top of the list covet your compliments on a daily basis. Those further down don't need so many, but a sincere, surprise compliment could really lighten their load. I put "neighbors" and "strangers" together because I'm a fan of the Good Samaritan story told by Jesus when he was asked, "Who is my neighbor?" This famous parable demonstrates that *your* actions and *your* mercy determine if a person is a stranger or a neighbor.[1] If you choose to treat someone with kindness, then you have become a neighbor to that person. No matter who crosses your path, you can either behave as a neighbor or a stranger. If you are neighborly, you simply won't see people as strangers.

When I was sixteen, standing in a cafeteria line, the woman dishing out the food looked up at me and brightly said, "I like your face" What a bizarre compliment! Usually a person comments on blue eyes or a nice smile. This lady just summed it all up with "your face!" But I loved it. In fact, it was probably *the* compliment that launched my strong feelings in this area. Since then, I've tried never to keep a compliment to myself. If I think something positive about a person, I say it out loud. I may be quiet about it, which is often appropriate. A loud, profuse compliment can make a person very uncomfortable. But I try never to be too shy to say simple things like, "Nice earrings" or "You are really funny" or "I like your face!"

If you read this whole book and the only thing you decide to do is to dole out compliments more freely, then you will be improving the lot of mankind and benefiting from this cheery component of the Social Cause Diet. Our words have the power to cause a great deal of damage; they can start forest fires, metaphorically speaking. But they also have the power to bring healing. "Pleasant words are a honeycomb, sweet to the soul and healing to the bones."[2]

---

1. The Good Samaritan story can be found in the book of Luke, chapter 10.
2. Proverbs 16:24, New International Version.

It is easier to build strong children than to repair broken men.

FREDERICK DOUGLAS

I've had years of selfishness. And I have to tell you, this is better....

DIANE KEATON, *on parenting*

If you want one year of prosperity, grow grain.
If you want ten years of prosperity, grow trees.
If you want one hundred years of prosperity, grow people.

CHINESE PROVERB

In Praise of Parent Volunteers

If you are a parent who helps out at your kids' school, you are hereby absolved of any additional volunteer responsibilities. That is, until they're in the fifth or sixth grade, when it would be an ideal time to explore various volunteer opportunities, bringing your kids along with you. But while they are still very young, it is likely that all of your hours of giving—and giving and giving and giving—will be spent on your family. Parenting well is your primary duty. As Winston Churchill said, "There is no finer investment for any community than putting milk in babies."

When my kids were young, I often contemplated how incredibly flexible, courageous and industrious volunteering parents have to be. It is not easy to go into a classroom of preschoolers, when you've had no special training, and help them cut and paste. Maybe it should be easy, but it isn't. It humbles us all—doctors, celebrities and otherwise competent people who all share similar challenges when they become moms and dads. Unless you've been a parent volunteer for a job that is out of your element, you can't imagine how challenging it can be.

If you're a mom who is feeling put off by it all, go to the library and check out *The Country Bunny* by Du Bose Heyward. This precious tale is about a bunny mom who sacrifices her dream job of delivering Easter eggs so that she can properly raise her babies. In the end, her dream comes true in a way that is only possible because of what she learned by being a parent. This children's book was published in 1939 and is reportedly taken from a story that was around for generations before that, so it's utter nonsense to think that there was ever a time when people found it easy to sacrifice for their children. Sacrifice has always been hard and always will be. But it's worth it. In the long run, you will be wiser, more fulfilled and more capable in all sorts of ways.

Incidentally, dads receive an added benefit when they show up as a volunteer, whether they choose to help in the classroom, coach a team, paint a preschool or serve at a science fair. The added benefit is that us moms will love you for it. We may not show it, but we are thrilled when dads work alongside us and volunteer on behalf of our kids. By the way, people may think it's easy for a dad to coach a team because—well—he's a man. Wrong! Coaching is quite a volunteer challenge, too. My friend once signed her husband up for a position as a soccer coach and wow, was he mad! After all, he knew nothing about soccer! He accepted the role begrudgingly. Fortunately, he became quite proficient at it, and—back to that added benefit—he earned a great deal of admiration from his wife.

On the other hand, there is a chance you can find a parenting volunteer job that comes naturally to you. When my kids were just entering the school system, I thought long and hard about what volunteer position I should accept. Before me was an intimidating list that described numerous responsibilities that needed filling. There was one–and only one–that seemed a good fit for me: *Parent Educator Coordinator.* As such, my responsibility would be to find, schedule and promote occasional speakers to inspire and educate our local parents. Since I have had the privilege of hearing many engaging speakers in my life, I felt confident I could pull this off. The job was indeed a good match and I kept it for six years!

One of the points of this book is to show there are agreeable ways for everyone to give. But as parents, it is necessary to do many jobs that are outside our comfort zone. We often have to throw *our* interests to the wind to help our children discover *their own.* Hopefully, you will find a few mom/dad jobs that suit you, but either way, it is your priority to serve your charges with attention, instruction, discipline and love while meeting their basic needs. When it comes to satisfying acts of service, there is no greater joy than that which comes from seeing your children flourish under your good care.

Quote by Diane Keaton from "Truly Madly Deeply" by Joanna Schneller. Copyright February 2008. Reprinted with the permission of *Ladies' Home Journal,* Meredith Corporation.

I wilt the lettuce
Spoil the meat
Rust the metal
Pothole the street
I devalue money
Deplete the time
I'm sorry, I'm sorry,
The shame is mine.

I litter the sidewalk
Pollute the air
Bloat my body
Thin my hair
I acid the rain
Oil the sea
I'm sorry, I'm sorry
It must be me.

GAIL JOHNSTON

The Complexities of Guilt

Guilt is complex. Guilty feelings, when they do their job well, cause us to take stock of our lives, fess up as needed, make changes for the better and do the right thing. Guilt has gotten a bad rap recently. Some people are so bothered with it, they drive around with "Screw Guilt" bumper stickers on their cars. Feelings of guilt can be harmful, but they can also be helpful. Sometimes they are a little of both! If you decide to try the Social Cause Diet because you'll feel guilty if you don't, while it's not the best reason, no one will complain and you'll still enjoy the benefits.

Where guilt does its damage is when we continue to feel condemned even after we've done our part in repentance and restitution, or when the offense or problem isn't our fault but we feel shame nonetheless. The poem I've included here was composed when I became aware of the nagging sense of guilt I carried around for all sorts of things. I tended to feel bad about one thing or another around the clock. In these extreme but not uncommon cases, one can try to reason with the negativity and bid it good riddance. Sometimes our inner parental voice simply needs to say, "That's enough already." But guilt can be stubborn. A guilt-ridden conscience may require the objective help of mature friends, pastors or counselors.*

If you are subject to guilt gone sour, be careful as you read the stories in the next section. They are meant to inspire you, not overwhelm you. They cover a whole gamut of services—you only need to get involved in one that works for you. There's no point in feeling bad about being uninvolved in the others. You can't possibly support all of these causes, and even if you could, we wouldn't want you to! All of us have our individual parts to play to make this a better world. You do your part, and I'll do mine.

A recent event in my life drove this point home to me. My

daughter is a ballet dancer. Like a good mom, I would volunteer to help backstage where I assisted little girls with their costumes and curls and lined them up to enter stage front at the proper times. After two years of this, I officially announced to myself and to anyone within earshot that I was not cut out for this job. I'm not quite sure why, but working behind the scenes unnerves me.

The next day, I received an enlightening call from my sister Jill, a person who happens to be a hero when it comes to meeting big needs. From serving the poor of the Appalachian Mountains to teaching autistic children to assisting people in hospice care, Jill has been there. But this day, she told me she had just finished a few weeks of doing something she considered rather frivolous: working in the wings for her daughter's school play. She discovered that she thoroughly loves showtime tasks such as whispering cues from the sidelines and pulling the curtains. Her exact words to me were, "Who would think I would find such fulfillment in this way?"

How perfect. How affirming to me and my decision *not* to serve in this way. The coincidental timing assured me that while I am not cut out for backstage volunteering, there are other people who are. I definitely do not need to push myself to be a stage mom. In fact, I should get out of the way and encourage others who may flourish in the role.

Another thing about guilt: if you are volunteering for those less fortunate than you, it's hard to come home and not feel guilty for all the things you have. For example, after a weeklong mission trip, there was talk in our group about going to a fancy restaurant. We were reluctant at first. The community we just served barely had enough to eat, and here we were choosing between a steakhouse and a bistro. But we decided to go for it and wound up having a warm, memorable time. The next time I was out there serving and the going got tough, I thought about that lovely dinner and was encouraged by the hope of another.

Debriefing after an act of service is critical for the purpose of interpreting our affluent environment in contrast to the limited resources of others. Should we downsize our house so we can give more money away? Or should we go out to dinner and reward ourselves for a job well done? These questions and the guilty feelings that often accompany them are valid. They require introspection and discussion with your significant others. If you have kids who are able to communicate, you may want to explore their thoughts. Once, when I was contemplating what was necessary versus what was extravagant in our lives, I asked my son—who was three at the time—what he thought. After a pause, he confidently announced, "All I need is a lawn and a tennis ball." A kid's perspective can be so refreshing.

After giving your questions and concerns adequate attention, you may decide to make some changes—or perhaps not. It is up to you and your loved ones to figure out. Once settled, guilty feelings should be diminished. The guilt has completed its important job of getting you to stop, think and make changes. Now it's time to move on—at least until you need to go through the process again.

There's something else to keep in mind as you consider the Social Cause Diet. We all have phases in our lives. Some phases may allow for more service than others. Be aware of what phase you are in, and don't feel guilty if you have to recede from volunteer service for a while to care for aging parents, for example, or because of a heavy work load.

Fortunately, more and more companies are providing opportunities for their employees to "give back," so even if you are in a demanding career, there's a chance you can experience satisfying acts of service on company time. If not on the job, consider serving on a holiday. Martin Luther King Day has skyrocketed as a national day of volunteer service. More than half a million Americans served in projects on MLK Day in 2008!

In addition, every service project needs people who offer encouragement, prayer and/or financial aid. If this is what makes up your variety of the Social Cause Diet due to time restraints, embrace your role with pride; nothing can happen without proper support.

I'd like to conclude this reflection by mentioning the feelings of guilt and shame that seriously interfere with productivity. I'm speaking of the frame of mind that tells a person he or she is too worthless (bad, sinful or flawed) to ever make a difference in the world. Some people struggle with this all their lives; others get hit with it now and then. Sometimes this guilt bellows in our ears, and other times it whispers words of self-condemnation. Either way, it is never worth listening to, never even remotely true.

Last summer, my friend Joel was in the midst of a divorce he didn't want. When a Christian youth camp asked him to be a counselor as he had been in the past, he felt too unworthy to accept the job. Thankfully, the camp persisted, and Joel went along, hanging his head pretty low. Although he felt better as the week progressed, he still wasn't convinced he had anything to offer. How could he when he had failed so gravely on the homefront?

During the last evening of the week, the campers were encouraged to approach the counselor of their choice if they had any concerns they wanted to discuss or prayer requests for their upcoming year. Although few responded, one teenager did approach Joel. The teen burst into tears of frustration and said that he didn't know what he should do with his life. Joel responded with a bit of amazement in his voice, "That's just how I feel!" They hugged, prayed together, and Joel explained that the boy needed to be patient—to keep seeking direction but to be patient; the answers will come. As soon as the boy left, another came up to Joel with a similar story. Again, Joel explained that he could relate to the boy perfectly. They prayed, shared some more, and Joel sent him on his way with words of encouragement.

No person should ever feel useless. As an advocate for the Social Cause Diet, I earnestly want everyone to know that they have something to offer, something others need.

In summary:

- Find a way to give of yourself and don't feel guilty about what you choose *not* to do.

- Examine any guilt you may feel in light of those less fortunate than yourself and determine what changes to make or not make, involving your significant others in the decision process.

- Never believe for a moment that you are too down or inadequate to contribute. In fact, sometimes it is out of the depths of despair that we find our efforts to be most effective, and we end up surprising ourselves with more compassion and commitment than we even knew we had.

---

*For a more complete discussion on the complexities of guilt, read *Shame and Grace: Healing the Shame We Don't Deserve* by Lewis B. Smedes.

Maturity is the ability to think, speak and act your feelings within the bounds of dignity. The measure of your maturity is how spiritual you become during the midst of your frustrations.

SAMUEL ULLMAN

Believable

A curious thing tends to happen when you increase your service to others. You might think that you would become more prideful and self-satisfied after doing a series of good deeds. Some people may choose to serve for the chief purpose of gaining that warm fuzzy feeling from knowing they were a part of making the world a better place. But what a person often acquires by becoming immersed in the needs of others is, instead, a trait called *humility*.

Humility is a positive trait, although it is largely misunderstood. It's best to explain what it *isn't* before elaborating on what it *is*. Having humility does not mean that you think you are weak or less important than others. It does not mean that you neglect taking care of yourself or consider yourself to be unworthy of grand pursuits and leadership positions. Nor does it mean that you listen to everyone else's ideas and fail to offer your own.

On the contrary, humility is knowing your rightful place in society, not thinking *too highly* of yourself or *too lowly* of yourself. It's when you understand your equality with others, how we are all human beings, freely given life—although some with more challenges than others. People are humbled when they serve because they identify with the person needing their help; they could just as easily have been on the receiving end of their service. They are humbled by the recognition that they have been spared themselves. They may also be humbled by the perseverance of those who are disadvantaged—how they carry on against the odds, while we who have so much tend to be complainers. Finally, they are humbled because no matter how much we contribute, there is more to do. We can't whip the world into shape; our efforts may make a huge difference, but, at the same time, they are a mere drop in the bucket. Humbly, we realize we need more time, more help, more resources, more prayer.

This increase in humility is a grand benefit. It helps us be receptive, approachable and teachable which is fertile ground for building relationships and for growth in all areas. It also leads to an attitude of gratitude—one of the finest traits a person can possess. Being humble goes hand in hand with being grateful—grateful for the abundance of what we have and grateful for the ability to give to others. Sure, we may have made good choices that put us in a position to share, but where did the wherewithal to make those good choices come from? Even our *will* is a gift. I am a highly motivated person, but I don't take credit for that. I realize that some people don't have that inner drive, and I thank God for my will and energy to get up and go. Summing up how this all relates to the Social Cause Diet, while you may expect to be impressed with yourself after a stint of social service, it's more likely you'll end up with a strong dose of humility and gratitude instead.

There are other emotions that surface in service—and life— less desirable ones like fear, anger and loneliness. A healthy person experiences a full range of emotions, yet we are often surprised and taken aback when the unpleasant ones enter the scene. In the "American Idol" series, the performers are often told that they are "believable" when they sing. What that means is that they sing with emotions we as the audience believe they really do feel. We believe they really do know the longing, pain, remorse, hope and love about which they are singing. And since we believe they have that inner depth and are singing from experience, we start to open up, allowing them to touch our own deep emotions and help us through them.

In our culture today, it's easy to be out-of-touch with our emotions. If we're feeling uncomfortable, we turn on the TV, turn up the music, exercise to oblivion, or find a substance to desensitize us. As previously disclosed, my substance of choice was food. Eating took away all my unpleasant emotions—temporarily, that is. In reality, they were still there, causing unease as they bristled under the surface. The final turning point in my recovery from my eating disorder came one morning when I woke up angry. It was run-of-the-mill anger at something mildly unfair that was going on at the office. But anger is uncomfortable and as usual, I immediately thought of getting something to eat. I felt urgent and *needed* to eat. But as I headed to the kitchen, I stopped myself, all of a sudden realizing that I wasn't *hungry*; I was *angry*. I sat down right there on the steps where it hit me, and told myself that it was okay to be angry, I just had to think it through. And it wasn't that bad! I didn't blow a fuse, I just felt angry. I don't remember if I came up with a solution to the problem or not, but I distinctively remember that I knew, *I knew* I was done stuffing my emotions down with food. I had recognized the pattern and had crossed over. I was excited...and no longer angry!

If you tend to hide from your emotions and have a low tolerance for the uncomfortable ones, try to remember just one simple fact: emotions won't kill you. No matter how sad you get, for example, you still have the power to say, "That's enough. I will move on." You really do. Tune into Dr. Laura on the radio sometime and she'll tell you all about it. This is an important truth to grasp for success in the Social Cause Diet because you may have fairly intense emotions in the service field. Did I mention that you might feel overwhelmed, fatigued and discouraged? But that's okay. Don't let these negative emotions deter you from offering aid. Acknowledge them, talk about them with others, journal about them, and keep going. Let your emotions *influence* your choices but not *rule* them. As you grow in your ability to understand your own emotions, you will also grow in your ability to understand those of others, too. You will thereby become more "human" and compassionate. Maybe some day you will be on stage, and people will even call you "believable."

2,000 Calories a Day

By now you've figured out that the Social Cause Diet isn't exactly about losing weight. The word "diet" is used here to mean anything that is an established habit or way of life. *Mrs. Smith has a steady diet of soap operas and game shows,* for example. Used in this broader way, we might analyze our diet by asking, "What do I do on a regular basis? Is my pattern of living healthy and satisfying, or is there something I am missing? What do I habitually hunger for, and does it fill me up when I get it?" The Social Cause Diet is about developing the habit of serving others for a healthier and more fulfilling life.

That said, if you need to drop a few pounds, application of the Social Cause Diet can help, as it did in a big way for Carolyn Escorico (see *Horse Sense and Weight Loss* on page 59). What you gain from volunteering—such as living more in the moment, making deeper connections with others, and growing in patience and gratitude— will make you a stronger, more contented person, thereby lightening your dependence on food. In addition, the satisfaction gained from serving others is truly filling, so the need to turn to food to fill one's emotional and spiritual cup is diminished.

But please know that I am well aware that there are wonderful, giving, self-sacrificial people who will retain weight no matter what. I in no way want to insinuate that they don't give enough! This book hopes to *free* people from the scales and from the constant effort to lose weight by emphasizing that there are better endeavors to pursue. Losing weight is not the most important thing in the world; yet when we start to focus on what *is* important, the pounds may very well fall away.

Nevertheless, if you are still looking for that perfect, practical diet tip, I would like to offer you the best one I have ever heard, one that has been backed up with solid research.

The particular study that impacted me involved three groups of people. Everyone was allowed 2,000 calories a day. One group was instructed to consume their allotment in the morning without eating anything else for the rest of the day. Another was told to consume all their food at lunchtime, another at dinnertime. The group that ate exclusively in the morning *lost* weight. The group that ate only at lunchtime *maintained* their weight. The group that ate everything in the evening *gained* weight.*

When I heard about this, I was already on the upswing. I no longer used food to avoid problems or stuff away emotions and was fairly well-adjusted, if I say so myself. But the study did catch my attention because the bulk of my calorie intake was still at night, with nothing but coffee in the morning. I wanted to make the shift, but it seemed drastic. How could I let go of my late night munchies? I decided I wouldn't let go of them right away, but I would start eating big breakfasts. In other words, I would go ahead and add the big breakfast without worrying about taking anything away at night.

My plan worked. Slowly but surely, I gave up my evening treats because I knew I was going to wake up to my favorite foods in the morning. If it was past ten or so at night and I wanted to start eating, I would tell myself, "Just go to bed. You can eat anything you want in the morning." Fortunately, doughnuts didn't appeal to me in the morning. At the start of the day, I was able to make great choices with foods like hearty cereal topped with walnuts, yogurt, and raisins.

Eventually, over the course of a year, I even lost those five extra pounds that I had always wanted to lose. And that was that—I've been the same weight for twenty years, give or take a few. Now my doctor says I'm too thin for someone my age. Oh brother. No one's perfect. I honestly feel like I eat everything I want. It's just that I don't *want* everything; I no longer turn to food when food is not the answer. I eat for sustenance and for the pure pleasure of it, but I don't eat to fill emotional, spiritual and social holes or to suppress feelings that are unpleasant.

Applying the breakfast plan concept to the Social Cause Diet, if you would like to add a healthy dose of service into your life but don't think you can give up anything in your schedule to make room for it, add the service anyway. Somehow, time seems to expand when we are doing the right thing. Try adding a service and see how it works out. Maybe you'll lose interest in a TV show so the service fits in easily after all. Maybe you'll find a project that involves physical activity, so you can miss your exercise class that day. Maybe you'll find something you can do while you're on the commuter train, like sew a smock for a preemie. Or maybe there's a service, like sponsoring a child, that actually doesn't take much time at all but makes an enormous difference in someone's life.

The stories that follow clearly do not represent *all* the services out there, but they demonstrate the *variety* of services. I hope they succeed in whetting your appetite for an ample portion of helping others in your own everyday life.

---

*Nancy L. Keim, Marta D. Van Loan, William F. Horn, Teresa F. Barbieri, and Patrick L. Mayclin. "Weight Loss is Greater with Consumption of Large Morning Meals and Fat-free Mass is Preserved with Large Evening Meals in Women on a Controlled Weight Reduction Regimen." *The Journal of Nutrition* 1997;127:75-82.

PART TWO

Stories of Satisfying Service

"People who serve often say,
'Thank you for the opportunity to be of service.'
They understand that their service to you
benefits themselves."

NIPUN MEHTA

Yancey

BY SHAUN GROVES

I grew up with the erroneous idea in my head that I was poor. I vowed that when I grew up I wouldn't be poor anymore. Not long after signing a record deal in 2000, the checks began to appear magically in my mailbox. And at the end of my third year of professional music making, we tallied up our winnings and discovered that I'd made, after taxes, almost $200,000. With a third child on the way and still feeling, for some unknown reason, as if we were living like almost-poor people, we designed and built our dream house—not as big as this guy's, not as fancy as that lady's, but what we thought was on the large end of middle-class.

Then two things happened. First, I took a job as co-pastor to young adults at my church where we taught from the book of Acts and then from the Sermon on the Mount. Acts 2 and Jesus' prayer in Matthew 5 made me shift in my seat and reevaluate my sacrifice-less faith.

Becky and I decided to sell our house and find something smaller and do other little things to cut down on spending, like cancel our cable. We decided to simplify our lives so that others could simply live. But, with the "for sale" sign in the front yard and no buyers calling, we wondered if we'd made the right decision.

Then I went to El Salvador.

There I met Yancey, a child we sponsored as a family through Compassion International. I pushed her in a swing. She rode on my shoulders through the marketplace and we shared a rainbow rocket pop. I traced her hand in crayon and she traced mine. I tickled her and she cackled just like my kids. We went to lunch and I bought her a hamburger. She only ate half and when I asked her if she was full she told me she wanted to save the rest so her little sister back home could eat it.

She fell asleep on the ride back to the hotel, her sweaty brown cheek squished up and buried in my t-shirt. And I prayed, asking God to forgive me for not giving away more of what he'd given me in my lifetime. "Forgive me" was all I could say holding a child who ate once every three days before Compassion International saved her life, educated her, and told her how much God loved her. Forgive me.

When Yancey kissed my cheek and told me good-bye at the bus stop that day, I knew I'd never miss my house or my cable again.

Our house sold and we moved into another down the street, less than half the size. We immediately received opportunities to use our extra wealth to help out those around us.

A bible study and a little girl flipped my life upside down. I'm not as worried now as I once was—I've seen the joy of the truly desperate and poor and believe their trusted God is my God, too. I don't want anything—I've had everything and been bored and thirsty for more, and I've had less and known passion and felt full. I'm not as easily upset—focusing my life on the third world has exposed the trivial trials of the first world for what they really are. I spend less—I see every starving child, their hair falling out, their tongues swollen and red, when I stand before a cash register. I know how much more they could use my money.

I think Compassion International should make their slogan: "Releasing Americans from wealth in Jesus' name." They do this. They gently, lovingly, pry the hands of the wealthy off the stuff we've labeled "mine" and use it to care for the poorest of the poor in the name of a God who says everything and everyone is his.

Read more by Shaun Grove, an insightful musician, writer and performer, by going to www.shaungroves.com. For child sponsorship, consider www.compassion.com.

I Call it Therapy

BY JANET HUCKABEE

My experience volunteering has been nothing short of a blessing. It helps me physically, emotionally and spiritually to help someone else. I call it therapy because I receive far more than I ever give.

During the horrible disaster of Hurricane Katrina, I found that a little help went a long way for the people who had lost everything. Many of them got relocated to our state and had no idea where they were when they got off the planes. They thought they were in Texas, but they were in Arkansas! They were very disoriented. Most didn't know anything about our state and didn't know where it was in reference to Louisiana. But when I told them that I was the first lady of Arkansas and that our people would take care of them, they believed me.

I went to each group that was seeking refuge and told them that I knew they had been through hell, but now they were going to experience a little piece of heaven. I prayed with each group that they would receive the care they needed. Then the other volunteers and I directed them to different places for shelter. We gave them maps, hugs, and warm meals, and they were truly comforted.

Helping someone is like wrapping a warm blanket around a new-born baby. It feels good and you know without a doubt it is the right thing to do.

Some of the most exciting times of my life have been when I've gotten together with a team of other women to build houses

THE SOCIAL CAUSE DIET

for single parents or struggling families. I enjoy doing things with my hands, framing, and working on the trusses and roof. I also like meeting and working with the family who is going to live there. At first, the man of the family is doubtful of us women, but then he quickly changes his mind after seeing us swing a hammer. That is always fun to watch. But the most rewarding part is interacting with the children in the families. Watching the expressions on their faces and seeing them jump up and down when the walls join together for their bedrooms is something more special than I can ever explain. For the first time in their lives, they will feel safe and protected from the outside world. What a joy for them and for me.

Attitude can make or break a volunteering experience. It is the key to a person's ability to be a great volunteer. The right attitude for a situation may be one of patience or confidence or honesty—or a combination of all three. Maybe, for some reason, the people you are giving to aren't grateful for your hard work. These are the times when you have to suck it up and maintain a positive attitude by remembering the times when people cried tears of joy because you helped them.

With a good attitude, everyone is blessed. Conversely, a bad attitude can ruin the whole moment. And it is a moment that you can never get back. One moment in time and forever you share it with the ones you want to help. It is not just your moment; it belongs to those around you as well.

Once I helped build a house for a little girl and her family. We had just installed the bathtub. The girl got so excited about having a bathtub that she got another worker and me to get in the tub with her and just sit there. We sat there in the tub, smiling. It is a one of my moments; it is one of her moments. And we will share it forever.

Former Arkansas First Lady Janet Huckabee says volunteering is the "glue" that holds our country together. She is Program Manager for American Red Cross of Little Rock, Arkansas and serves on the Board of Directors for Habitat For Humanity International.

Horse Sense and Weight Loss

BY CAROLYN ESCORICO

I've always been funny. It goes without saying that if you're a fat girl, you've got to be funny. While my proclivity for good humor has served me well, the fat hasn't. Especially when I topped 300 pounds.

You would think I knew something about rejection, having been overweight all my life, but when the local private school rejected my son Ethan, I felt pain on his behalf like none I have ever experienced. My family had just relocated to a new neighborhood to be close to this reportedly wonderful school, only to be informed that my son's case of ADHD was too much for them. My husband and I had adopted Ethan, a "drug baby," seven years earlier and his developmental challenges were becoming overwhelming for us all.

Then Ethan's counselor suggested a horse therapy program. While Ethan struggled to be socially up to par with people, he was a natural with animals—more than once, a bird has been known to land on him. So we visited SonRise Equestrian Foundation and I was given a chair by the stables to sit in and observe. This was good so far. You see I couldn't just leave Ethan at the farm and risk another incident in rejection—we were both so wounded. I needed to be there, watching, in case Ethan needed an interpreter or in case people got impatient with him.

Such fears turned out to be unfounded in this place; everyone there was so calm, accepting, and intuitive that Ethan began to shine in no time. I suppose I could have left him there without me in subsequent visits, but something kept me around. I discovered that I needed these people—and horses—in my life too.

Prior to this time, I had only seen horses in pastures on the side of the road while driving by. When I got up close to them, I was really scared. So I preferred to stay put in my chair and watch. The only thing is, there are a quite a few arenas and round pens at this horse barn and Ethan did a lot of hiking about. To follow him, I had to leave my chair and climb a small mountain. Actually, it was only a slight incline, but with the weight I was carrying, it was a mountain. While everyone else would bound up it, I would walk a few labored steps, then stop and rest. Four times I would have to do this before reaching the top. I would stop, look around and pretend I was merely pausing to enjoy the lovely environs as I caught my breath.

But I persevered, and it eventually got a little easier to peruse the grounds and I got more comfortable with the horses. Then these nice people—I'm sure for my benefit more than theirs—asked if I would like to be a volunteer and help work with the horses. This would entail that I walk horse after horse up the "mountain" and then run them around in circles in the round pen. I asked them, "Couldn't I please just sweep the barn instead?" But they thought I could actually do this work and they wanted to teach me how. After a few weeks of lessons, I officially became a horse handler volunteer— all 309 pounds of me.

Thus it started to happen. With all the walking, the pounds began to drop. The exercise was obviously what I needed, but also the opportunity to do something worthwhile. My existence before the horse farm was pretty lame—if I wasn't taking care of the kids, my life consisted of eating, sleeping and doing laundry. Now I had something to do that pretty much gave me everything: exercise, good company, challenge and purpose. On top of it all, I was witnessing a transformation in my son who now had a best friend and was doing well in the public school.

Today I'm a full 102 pounds less than I was that first visit to the farm when all I could do was sit in the chair. No doubt I'll continue to lose more weight while I stay in this healthy environment. And stay I will, since I just acquired my very own horse! My life has opened up for me like never before. When I escort my horse to the open pasture so he can buck, snort and enjoy his freedom with the other horses, I realize I am feeling pretty free myself. I've seen it happen for other families in this program too. Although their circumstances are different, they find similar healing.

When I think about it, I suppose it wasn't just the wonderful community of the horse barn that saved me. I suppose I had to do something too. I had to open up and risk trusting these people, even on the heels of the serious rejection I had experienced. I also had to accept their trust in me, a fat girl, and consider that maybe I did have something to offer. Basically, I had to climb a mountain. It was a serious mountain to me at the time, but in my slimmer condition, I see it for what it really is—a gentle slope—and I bound up and down it with a horse at my side about 40 times a day.

"Loving Children through Crisis and Helping Horses in Need." SonRise Equestrian Foundation is a nonprofit organization making a positive difference for children with social, emotional and physical needs, including terminal illnesses. Participating children develop confidence, integrity and responsibility through mentoring and peer relationships centered around the care and enjoyment of horses. Visit www.sonriseequestrianfoundation.org for more information.

A Fashionable Service

BY TRISTON MCLAUGHLIN

As I am taking photos of my daughter Cara, laughing with her friends who are similarly adorned in long dresses, we give each other a wink. We are both thinking about our volunteer work with The Princess Project. It ended a month earlier, but it is still with us. As I look at Cara's pretty friends, I feel so proud and happy that, as part of The Princess Project, we were able to help hundreds of other girls less fortunate than us also have a special dress for the rite of passage known as *prom*.

It all started when Cara, 15 at the time, was looking for a service project for school. We had both done lots of volunteer work before, but we were hoping to find something to do together this time. We were also looking for something in line with my daughter's passion—fashion. Then we discovered The Princess Project—an amazing organization in the Bay Area of San Francisco that provides a prom dress free of charge to any high school girl who needs one.

We spent our first day with The Princess Project at its downtown "store," which consisted of three floors of an old office building. It was an unusual, rather awkward space right in the middle of Market Street. We pushed around clothes racks and sorted hundreds and hundreds of beautiful dresses and accessories by size and color. Then the next Saturday, we did it again! Another overflowing supply of dresses needed to be sorted and checked for quality. The variety and prettiness of the dresses were astounding. They were never more than five years old, all dry cleaned and dressy, from size 0-22, acquired from collection drives at schools and gyms or donated by manufacturers and fashion designers.

Each Saturday, my daughter and I spent hours there. We met other volunteers who gave their time way beyond what we did and others who came for just the day. There were teen groups and clubs who also came to sort dresses and help decorate the store to create a wonderful shopping experience for each and every girl who came to look for a dress.

Those times with Cara were so much fun: getting up early, taking the subway downtown, chatting, having breakfast in the local diner, and then working together for others. Sometimes we worked in the same area; other times we had different jobs. Tasks included untangling necklaces, breaking down boxes for recycling, or going over donated dresses to make sure they were in excellent condition. It was a joy to see my daughter, who at the time was hunting down her own prom dress, take so much pride in this cause. She knew that each dress represented a girl who wasn't as lucky as she was—who might be from a group home, a foster family, or a family who can't make ends meet but still wants to see their beautiful high school girl go to her prom looking amazing. Cara knew that for a girl, a large part of the memories that make up prom is feeling pretty all night long, as well as the preparation leading up to it—looking for the perfect dress, choosing accessories, getting ready with friends, and receiving that priceless attention from those who cared.

"Thank you so much for the dress. I couldn't go to prom without it." "Thank you for being so nice and helping me find the exact dress I wanted." "The personal attention was amazing. I want to help next year!" These were typical responses on the cards the girls filled out after they found their dresses. As Cara and I read the comments aloud to each other, we both teared up. We didn't know any of the circumstances that brought the girls to that downtown office that was converted into a prom mecca, just that they had found their way there. They were referred by counselors, group home staff, radio talk shows, foster parents, or friends who got their dresses there in years past. Some shopped alone, some shopped with groups, but each and every girl had a volunteer there to give her individualized attention. Almost all the girls went away with a dress, and everyone got a goodie bag with an accessory, donated makeup, and more.

Back to my daughter's prom. She is so beautiful and happy. As significant as this event is for her, it is now much bigger, knowing that she played a part in helping other girls feel pretty and happy, at least for the one very important night of prom. My daughter is not just thinking about herself; she now knows how much she has to offer others. And what we both came away with from The Princess Project was precious time together that is so rare these days and pride in a job well done.

There are many organizations around the country that provide free prom dresses. Visit www.princessproject.org and go to the Resources section for links to find one near you.

Two Thumbs Up

BY CODY FISHER

I raq is relentless. Just when you try to have a positive attitude or start fresh, you walk out the door and immediately new struggles are thrown at you. The culture hits you from one angle, no electricity from another angle, having to walk through the cold to find a taxi from yet another.

Yesterday I ran into a man who is simply crazy. Everybody knows him. He's mentally not there and most people just laugh at him. He came up to talk to me with a fat cigar in his mouth. Between the clouds of smoke in my face I could see the biggest smile on his. He was full of joy and happiness. Was he on something? I don't know. I've seen him before and he has always been this happy. He was wearing the same clothes he wore weeks ago but it only seems to bother the people who can smell him. I love this guy. He brought so much light into my day.

Not even five minutes later I ran into another guy probably my age or a bit younger. He was deaf and mute. He was using his hands to communicate in the language he had created. Next to the crazy guy, he was the happiest person I've seen in months. The one thing I could understand was the thumbs-up he continued to give me. Then he pulled out a piece of paper from his pocket and handed it to me. It was a Doctor's report on his condition. Most of it was in Kurdish but there was one line in English, the one line he seemed to want to know about. It said "Deaf and Mute…absolutely no treatment or cure."

After a series of motions, somebody next to him told me that he wants to know if he can fly to America and get treatment. I pointed to the paper and told them what it said. Try communicating to a deaf and mute guy by using your hands that there's no treatment for him. His motions stopped and he became somber for about a minute. Then his head popped up along with his two thumbs and he started to smile all over again.

How come a crazy homeless man and a deaf and mute with no treatment possible were the two happiest people I met yesterday? What's more ironic…them being full of joy or somebody like me struggling to find it? I'm not sure but I'm telling you right now—I want to be more like them today, not me.

Cody Fisher and Jeremy Courtney founded Buy Shoes. Save Lives., a nonprofit that sells hand-made Iraqi shoes and gives the profits to fund heart surgeries for Iraqi children. Visit www.buyshoessavelives.com.

My First Avon Breast Cancer Walk

BY MICHELLE BERMAS

It's two days, thirty-nine miles and its intimidated me for years. The Avon Walk for Breast Cancer is an incredible cause and a huge accomplishment for anyone who participants. One of their slogans is, "Every three minutes someone is diagnosed with Breast Cancer." Though I've never had any direct experience with the disease, I have friends who've survived it and others who have lost their mothers because of it.

Despite a strong interest, the two things that stopped me from signing up were fear of collapsing at mile two and the fundraising. Walkers must raise $1,800 to participate. As a reluctant fundraiser, I'd rather write a check from my bank account and be done with it. Unfortunately, that's not remotely possible with my financial situation.

It was the constant, trademark pink television and magazine ads for the Boston Walk that encouraged me to act. I gathered my confidence and attended an introduction meeting at the library. Other potential walkers were as concerned as I was about raising the money. That's when I heard the phrase "Fearless Fundraising." The speaker brainstormed ideas such as yard sales, craft fairs, bake sales, theme parties and car washes. Her best advice? Do not decide who can afford to donate to you and who couldn't. Just send out your donation request letters to everyone you know explaining why you were walking.

In an excited move I signed up, still wary about the fundraising but believing that I could make a difference. After setting up my web site and sending out letters, I watched money trickle in. It was a fascinating study to see who donated and how quickly. It was exactly like the Avon staff said; don't decide ahead of time because you'll be surprised who'll respond and how much they'll donate. Dollar by dollar I made my goal. It felt exhilarating to raise that much money when in the beginning, I wasn't sure if I'd pass the hundred dollar mark. Anything is possible if you take it step by step—literally.

Walkers were required to check in on Friday night for Event Eve in Boston. I live on the South Shore, twenty minutes from the city (without traffic) and one hour when it's a parking lot. I decided taking the subway would be easier. My friend Doreen (one of the women I was walking for) dropped me off at the station. She gave me excellent directions that any normal person could follow. I hopped on the subway headed to Boston and felt like a city girl for about twenty seconds.

Why was my train moving backwards?

That's when I learned that the subway won't stop, even if you shout, "Crap, we're headed the wrong way!" and bang on the glass doors. They're sticklers like that. Also, I wouldn't advise stuffing a twenty dollar bill into the subway ticket machine…unless you want eighteen dollars spit back in coins. All I can say is I'm not a fan of mass transit. Especially since I had to haul my suitcase (only one allotted per walker, not to exceed thirty pounds which included one sleeping bag, one sleeping mat, two ponchos, two pairs of sneakers and clothing) through Boston and on to the event.

The weekend of the walk it rained as if Noah was in town. Our weather choices: rain, hard rain, spritzing, misting and…do I see animals walking two by two?! Luckily our tent was *almost* waterproof. Since it was my first time sleeping in one, I learned two things: 1) The walls are not sheetrock and 2) Streams are pretty and quaint, but not when they're running alongside my sleeping bag. Then there was that little hot water issue when I showered at 8:30 p.m. Even the port-a-potties+poncho+fanny pack was an adventure. But the mud made me sad. It smelled like wet dog and had a habit of oozing inside your shoes, making you say, "Whoops a daisy" as you fell backwards.

At 3 a.m. I had to go potty, thanks to the trickling stream taunting my bladder. I tried to be quiet for Alison, my tent mate. Instead, I felt like a 300 pound grizzly inside a bag of potato chips. I unzipped our tent to get out, "ZZZZZIPPPPP!" Then I placed one foot out and into the sludge, where it sank, creating a suction cup effect. I did the crab walk, hoping to propel my horizontal body like a gymnast so it would land upright outside the tent, but vertical didn't quite happen.

Did I mention there is nothing uglier than a poncho? It's not like I was trying to make a fashion statement but I looked like I was headed off to the rainforest with a pink Hawaiian lei, necklace and beads. Sure, I'm a hottie, I can pull it off, but what about the other 2,799 chicks?

You know that saying about eating an elephant one bite at a time? Well, that's how I walked seventeen miles on Saturday and thirteen miles on Sunday. I used to fear this walk. I was too fat, too out of shape, wouldn't raise the money, and would never be able to keep up. Now it doesn't seem so scary to do it again. (Although I still circle the block looking for the closest parking spot at my YMCA. Ironic, isn't it?)

On a serious note, the generosity of people was amazing. Whenever I got discouraged, fellow walkers pushed me onward. Little old ladies came out of their houses in their pajamas to clap and say, "Thank you." The crew of motorcycle men, cheering vans and bicyclists really helped. They strapped pink bras to their vehicles and kept us moving with compliments and reassurance.

The miles weren't marked so it was a relief to hear them say,

"Only two more miles until lunch" or "Good job, you're at mile ten." At one point they told us we were at mile eleven. Later on, they said, "Good job. You're at mile nine." At the rate we were walking, we'd be back to the starting line in no time.

The whole time I was thinking, "I don't want to come in last, I don't want to be last." But thanks to training, I came in hours ahead of schedule. Once across the finish line, Alison and I cheered other walkers and danced in the rain to the rock music. And you know what? The last group of walkers stopped at a bar to celebrate, that's why they were last! Of course it didn't matter about being last, just about doing it.

So thanks to my friends and supporters, I raised $2,205. This accomplishment means a lot to me, and now I'm dreaming of even bigger goals for myself. I was just one of the 2,800 walkers and fearless fundraisers. Collectively we raised over six million dollars.

At the end of it all, a stranger put a homemade heart necklace around my neck and said, "My daughter was your age when she died of breast cancer. Thank you for walking."

 Michelle Bermas enjoys life with her husband, two kids and a white lab who eats the couch. She's been published in the 2008 Writer's Market. For a Avon Walk near you, go to www.avonwalk.org.

Writing for the Cure

BY ELIZABETH FISHEL

Nine doors will close in your face," my father always taught me, "before the tenth one opens." As I hit mid-life with the new millennium, my ears buzzed with the harsh finality of slamming doors. My mother died after a long, grueling battle with breast cancer. My older son got ready to leave home for college three thousand miles away. My latest book came out into which I had poured four years of work and high hopes; despite good reviews, it did not exactly fulfill my fantasies of bestsellerdom and early retirement. Staring at those closed doors, I felt stuck. Night after night, I'd wake into the unforgiving glare of 3 a.m., restless with hormones and self-doubt, and toss and turn until dawn. "Necessity is the reinvention of mother," was an essay I started to write but, no surprise, could never quite finish. I dreamed of reinvention, I hungered for it, but I didn't know where to begin.

Still, once a week, every Wednesday, I put my own stalled plans aside to guide a group of women writers along their literary journey, to nurture their dreams. Like a therapist who struggles with personal demons but still keeps appointments with patients, I showed up. For ten years, I met with these twelve or so women of all ages and life-stages who gathered in my living-room to hone their craft. Part writing class, part support group, part literary salon, our writers' community had a core of members who stayed for the long haul while others came for a session or two and moved on, making room for new blood. In other worlds they were doctors and lawyers, therapists and publicists, mothers taking time out from child-raising to probe their own thoughts, claim their own voices. Sinking comfortably into sofa and arm-chairs, sipping strong coffee or peppermint tea, we aired and shared our dreams and doubts and learned what it meant to write from the heart. We stuck together through marriages and divorces, babies and grandbabies, career shifts and retirement, illness and recovery, transforming our "diamonds in the dustheap"—in Virginia Woolf's famous phrase—into all varieties of first-person writing.

Most of the women were unpublished when they joined the group, writing first for pleasure and self-revelation. I preached the joys of process over product and stressed the sloppy first draft. The difference between published and unpublished, I promised, was fanny-on-chair perseverance. I told them to strap themselves to their desk chairs by the sash of their bathrobes, if necessary, as John McPhee once confessed that he did. Then I pushed them to polish draft after draft until they shined. "No writer gets it right the first time" became our group's mantra.

One by one the writers who were ready started sending out their work for publication. I dusted off my father's words of wisdom. "Nine doors will close in your face," I told them, braced for those inevitable first rejections, standing by with Kleenex—and extra mailing envelopes. Then gradually, as I knew it would, that tenth door started creaking open for a few of them. One writer entered a local bookstore's annual travel-writing contest and won first prize, a plane ticket to anywhere in the world. A few started appearing in local newspapers with pieces on the Mideast conflict, the roots of terrorism, and other global hot buttons. And two women who'd never published a word pitched a column idea to their suburban paper and got the job—a bimonthly column they wrote together called "Double Talk." Those first by-lines inspired us all.

Little did I imagine that helping midwife these fellow writers' dreams would help me get back my own. We called ourselves the

"Wednesday Writers" and we were all women on the cusp, women in transition, drawn to the group to make sense of life passages and upheavals. We were mining our inner lives, first to understand ourselves better, then to reach out and resonate with others. "The personal life deeply lived," wrote Anais Nin, "goes beyond the personal." We wrote for our own survival and to prove this larger mission true.

Meanwhile the shadow of breast cancer darkened our intimate circle, mirroring the national epidemic. Mothers, sisters, friends and a sobering handful of our writers coped with it, wrote about it, and did their best to carry on. During the ten years we had been meeting, the lives of two of our members were cut short by cancer.

Then my mother died. Watching her valiant three year struggle against this relentless opponent filled me with roiling emotions that matched the complexities of our relationship—admiration, sadness, fear, powerlessness. After she died I felt so hollow and removed, I understood why mourning women in other cultures cloaked themselves in black robes. It was protective armor: "Don't come too close or expect too much of me," it announced. For weeks after her death, the only writing I did was answering condolence notes.

But eventually, after months of mourning, I knew I had to transform my grief into something positive. My mother had been a doer, a talented multi-tasker—professional ceramicist, avid tennis player, financial whiz, ardent traveller. Her letters, full of family news and mother-wisdom, were characteristically signed not "Love" or "Yours," but "Rushing." She also knew how to worry a problem until a solution emerged. In her honor, I knew I needed to plan a course of action, a way to make a difference for other breast cancer patients, some means of raising money to battle this devastating disease that took too many precious lives.

Inspiration came quickly, spawned as I mused about the fundraising marathons that raise money and attention for a variety of worthy causes. For several years, my mailbox had overflowed with requests from friends putting their bodies on the line for heart disease, leukemia, ALS. But since I didn't run or bike or even walk huge distances, I wanted to use the one skill I could sustain for long periods of time—writing. Not logging miles but spinning words would be my contribution.

With relief I realized that I would not have to tackle this write-athon alone. I approached my circle of Wednesday Writers, and we mobilized quickly with a two step fundraising plan. We planned a day-long literary event at the University of California/San Francisco Medical Center, "Healing Words," that would feature readings by acclaimed writers, as well as breast cancer survivors sharing their own experiences. And there we would launch an anthology of our essays and continue to sell it with all proceeds donated to the UCSF Breast Care Center. Welcome seed money came from the hospital's auxiliary who believed in our project when it was just a gleam in our eye.

Collective energy plus tenacity and ingenuity fueled the project from the get-go. We started by e-mailing all the writers who'd been in the group for the past ten years and gave each of them the chance to submit first-person essays for the book. We chose the best of their best and we also included stories by our two members who had died. The resulting anthology, *Wednesday Writers: Ten Years of Writing Women's Lives,* which I co-edited with Terri Hinte, is a poignant collection of work on family and identity, love and loss, illness and recovery, and the daily pleasures and surprises of ordinary life. Touching universal themes, each of us had written from the emotional center and reached for the reader's heart. What emerged is a portrait of contemporary women, resonant, complex and well-rounded.

Engrossed in our project, busy and engaged, I gradually began to heal from my midlife malaise. The details of organizing and editing the manuscript eclipsed the creative doubts, and the company of thirty other women captivated me more than navel-gazing. When I woke in the middle of the night, I'd go over the details of our book instead of numbering my own flaws and failings. Soon, I stopped waking altogether, and my days revved up with renewed energy.

In a couple of months we had edited, organized, formatted, and dispatched the book to a local printer, just in time to be received for our "Healing Words" fundraiser. No first edition was ever more cherished, no longed-for baby more coddled by its thirty-plus godmothers.

The combination of passionate personal writing by a group of ordinary women, most never before published, and the book's goal as a fundraiser for breast cancer research touched a nerve in northern California with ripples nationwide. A month after publication, for two weeks running, *Wednesday Writers* appeared on *The San Francisco Chronicle's* Bay Area paperback bestseller list, galloping right behind *Seabiscuit*. Terrific media attention followed with features and glowing write-ups in a multitude of local publications. Spring, summer, fall, we were booked solid with readings and events, a heady fifteen minutes of fame for all of us.

So while I'd been knocking on nine other doors, *Wednesday Writers* proved to be the tenth. The camaraderie and shared pleasures of our collaborative effort energized me out of my midlife doldrums, and contributing to an important cause gave me a sense of larger purpose and focus; in contrast, my own problems down-sized to a manageable scale. Professionally, I reaped the benefits of the book's positive trickle-down. Our many public appearances and media coverage brought the group welcome attention, and new writers clamored to join. My Wednesday Writers' group got so full that I now have a Friday session as well. Invitations to do readings and give talks have me back in circulation, revitalized and with a new subject I feel passionate about.

As for my abandoned essay on reinvention? I managed to finish it just in time to include it in *Wednesday Writers*. This time a door had barely closed before I could hear it swinging open again to let in the fresh breeze of something new.

In 2007, Elizabeth Fishel co-edited (with Terri Hinte) a second Wednesday Writers anthology, *Something That Matters: Life, Love, and Unexpected Adventures in the Middle of the Journey*. She is also the author of four nonfiction books, including *Sisters* and *Reunion: The Girls We Used To Be, The Women We Became*. For more information, visit www.wednesdaywriters.com.

Mbali

BY DR. MAITHRI GOONETILLEKE

Lindiwe had spunk! Even though she had only danced this earth for four tender years, she knew somewhere deep inside, that she was born to strut. And man, she did. Like a little bird of paradise, completely comfortable in the seat of her power and the knowledge of her beauty.

But it was her best friend, Mbali, who I was concerned about.

Mbali, with her big bambi eyes and brown porcelain face, would never speak unless she was spoken to.

At lunch time after clinic, I'd go down to the pediatric ward to play endless games of hopscotch and 'give me 5' and sing songs with my favorite choir of angels dressed in their blue hospital gowns, but Mbali's joy was always contained.

When I asked her how she was, she would whisper "I am fine" and turn her head to her feet.

So every day, I would call a nurse to my side to translate for me the same words, "Mbali, you are a beautiful young girl. And what's more, your voice is beautiful. It is a gift given to you from heaven. You must never be afraid to speak to anyone. You must stand tall and proud, and say 'I am Mbali, and my voice is beautiful.'"

And she would stand and whisper in the softest Si Swati, "I am Mbali and my voice is beautiful," and I would put my hands to my ears like the clown I am and pretend that I couldn't hear, "What? I am sorry, I am old and deaf. What was that you said?"

One day I was in the hospital cafeteria where a group of nurses were talking and I overheard one of them say, "So when I told her it was time to stop playing and come take her medicine she said, "I am Mbali, and my voice is beautiful."

Even my toes were smiling.

Did you know that the number one most accurate predictor of a nation's infant mortality rate, is the proportion of woman who are educated in that country?

Please take a moment to take this in.

Any doctor who works in the field of international health will tell you the same.

Community health is directly proportional to the empowerment and the education of women.

If we want humanity to move forward; if we want there to be less suffering and disease in the world, then we cannot afford to allow the subjugation of women to continue.

Furthermore, I believe every man in this world, needs to stand up and fight for the rights of our sisters, our mothers, our lovers, our female friends across the length and breadth of our planet. Till there is true equality.

To read more by Dr. Maithri Goonetilleke, visit www.soaringimpulse.blogspot.com. Maithri would also like to refer you to www.thehungersite.com and www.freerice.com.

Before Their Time

BY MICHAEL WHITMAN

When tragedy strikes, the possibility that we will ever emerge from the pit of despair seems remote. As we look up, we see only a small circle of blue sky, almost blotted out by the surrounding darkness. Eventually, though, the circle of sky grows larger and the darkness becomes less overpowering. Even so, it can still seem impossible that any good will ever emerge from this event.

Some years, later, however, I began to understand advice that had seemed absurd when it was first offered: "Look for the gift in this." Eventually, I came to see that something of value could in fact be discerned.

My family went through the devastating experience of losing our 23-year-old son Breck to suicide in 1994. My wife and I had done the best parenting we could, but unfortunately, we knew nothing about the warning signs of suicide. If we had been more knowledgeable, could we have prevented it?

A late-night telephone call told me what had happened, and my knees buckled. The phone started making rude, blaring noises in my hand, but I didn't want to hang it up and break that imagined final connection.

How different from my reaction to my elderly father's death! That event was rather like the gentle closing of a long, deeply appreciated book, but Breck's suicide was like having my heart torn from me. Suddenly, the future of this young person who had so much going for him, so much for us all to look forward to, disappeared.

Only one day after our town began to hear about our loss, a close friend asked my wife and me to come to her house so she could give us something before we flew to California (where Breck had been living) for the funeral. Sydney Long is both a pianist and a composer, and she sang for us "Breck's Song," which had come to her within hours of hearing about his death. The depth of this song and Sydney's grasp of what a parent feels in this unique situation simply stunned us. She recorded a demo tape for us, and her beautiful song continued to comfort and soothe me during the long flight and for weeks later.

Anyone who has mourned a traumatic death knows that people lean on a variety of aids, supports, rituals, and crutches to get them through the first weeks. We each grieve in our own ways. What works for one may make grieving more difficult for another. What worked for me was music. I have always loved beautiful melodies and lyrics, so to cope with my grief, I often put on headphones, went off by myself, and let music work its comforting magic.

In addition to Sydney's song, I listened to "Tears In Heaven," Eric Clapton's deeply moving memorial to his very young son who died in a fall. Long-familiar songs also took on poignant meaning for me, two of which were Jackson Browne's "For A Dancer" and "Empty Chairs at Empty Tables," from *Les Misérables*. Hearing these songs sent tears down my cheeks, but I understood that this was an essential part of the healing process. I would probably shed a gallon eventually, so whatever started them flowing was okay.

Four years after Breck died, an idea sprang into my head for a project that I immediately wanted to explore. Knowing how much comfort music had brought me, I fastened onto the idea of producing a CD of memorial songs that would help others deal with tragic loss. I knew it should be titled *Before Their Time,* and although I had never been involved in such work, my enthusiasm was stronger than my ignorance.

Off I went, inexperienced but convinced that since such a

collection had never before been compiled, it needed to be done and I was the person to do it. I used to be shy about asking people for donations, but because this was the only way my project would fly and I believed in it so much, cold-calling for funding and for asking musicians for permission to include their songs proved to be easy. I sought all materials and services *gratis,* so it took a whole year to get everything in hand for the album. In the year 2000, the first CDs arrived. Any author, musician, or producer tells of the same thrill, when all that work is behind you and you finally hold the real thing in your hand. I was elated.

Little did I know that publicizing, marketing, and actually selling the CDs would be a much longer and grueling task. This was not the fun part, but I discovered that giving lectures, which I call "Music To Lean On," would be a far more effective and enjoyable way to promote the CDs than traditional advertising. I gained a large audience among medical and mental healthcare professionals who seldom get to grieve over the patients they lose as part of their work. They had no idea that there is such a wide and deep vein of music that can provide comfort and consolation.

While I never could have landed a job as the producer of a major album, as a volunteer on a mission, I became the executive producer of a total of three volumes of *Before Their Time,* a project that has now contributed over $50,000 in net revenue to various foundations, including the American Foundation for Suicide Prevention and the NH Youth Suicide Prevention Assembly. Many great works have been originated by philanthropists who start off ignorant about the logistics of a project, but are led by strong and pure inspiration.

Great loss was my inspiration. I was advised by a few people in the music industry that *Before Their Time* was too difficult a task—that it would never make a dime. But I persevered and, at each stage, I learned what needed to be done and how to do it. Now these musical collections are available to everyone who is mourning a painful loss.

Equally important, due to the success of these CDs, I've become deeply engaged in statewide programs to increase community awareness of the risk factors and warning signs of suicide. While I will never know whether or not my wife and I might have prevented the suicide of our own son, I am now helping teenagers, other parents, and caring adults know what to look for, so that, as far as it is up to us, young people will choose to live out their futures.

Michael Whitman is a producer and a lecturer on the role of music in the healing process. To order *Before Their Time*, visit www.beforetheirtime.org.

No Lunch for Lent

BY SEAN BLOMQUIST

One of the best things I have been a part of in our church community is nothing new to our orthodox tradition, but it was a new experience for us this year. During the season of lent—a time of reflection and preparation for Easter—we decided to partake in the ancient practice of *fasting*. Although fasting can be done alone, it is often a communal experience. Our church decided to fast together for two weeks by giving up one meal a day and refrain from dining out. This partial fast was realistic but still challenging for our culture of well-fed individuals.

The exciting thing about our lenten exercise was that we were not only giving *up* something, but we were also giving *to* something. First of all, we were giving to others through prayer. The time we would ordinarily spend eating, we spent in prayer. If you believe in the power of prayer, this added up to a lot of power.

In addition, since we were each saving five to ten dollars a day on food, we decided to give that money away. We contacted an organization in Africa called AHEAD, and they told us that the money we were saving was enough to support a family of six in Liberia for an entire year, providing them with food, medical coverage, education for their children and even a house.

During the fast, I felt a real change taking place in my own life as I thought about my own consumption and how two weeks of mild sacrifice could make such a major difference to someone else. I also began to feel a deep connection to our global community, knowing that the choices I was making would affect others so far away.

Our church succeeded in our goal, sending $2,400 to the family AHEAD picked for us. The family happened to be that of a pastor and a beautiful match—our service to this one pastor will, in turn, impact many others as he will be able to serve his community for an entire year, knowing that the needs of his own family are being met. Hopefully, we will pull off the fast again next year, and the service will go on.

Sean Blomquist has three lively children, one exceptional wife, and two usually bare feet. For information on AHEAD Ministries, visit www.aheadministries.org. If you would like to read more stories from Sean's church, visit www.shelteronline.org.

In Concert with my Dad

BY ELIZABETH STOOKEY SUNDE

Is it really volunteering when you're the daughter of a social activist? Sometimes volunteering doesn't really feel like a choice. Sometimes it's what you do because you sense such a clear need for something to be done and you're not sure who else might do it. Or an opportunity presents itself, even casually, and you realize that you have been given a chance to make a difference, so you step in.

You would know my Dad best as Paul of the folk trio, Peter, Paul and Mary. He is a loving, kind, smart, funny man who also happens to have been relatively famous at one point in his life, and he still lives on in history books and people's memories as a visionary for world peace and social justice. When people would ask me some silly question like, "Do you sing as well?" I would always respond, "Yes, but not as well as my Dad," and leave it at that.

My father and I always had a great relationship, but I didn't expect that our vocational paths would ever have an opportunity to cross. There was no way I thought I could follow in his footsteps after the enormous role he had played on the international stage.

In late 1997, I was just married and launching my own nonprofit management practice in New York City. During a casual conversation, Dad asked whether, some day, I might consider taking over the Public Domain Foundation (PDF) he had created for the purpose of distributing all royalties from his divinely inspired "Wedding Song" to charity. (You've likely heard this timeless song, describing the union of marriage, that Dad wrote as a blessing for the wedding ceremony of his fellow folksinger, Peter Yarrow.)

And just like that, an opportunity presented itself that I felt I couldn't refuse and which has and could very well continue to change my life forever. Because I said, "Yes, Dad, I would be very interested in taking charge of this foundation—not at some point in the future—but right now so you'll be by my side as we build it!"

The foundation I was inheriting actually had no money in the bank. Its only asset was one song, albeit one that generated between $20,000-$40,000 a year. Dad had not been advised to create an endowment so the money earned each year was given away, in its entirety, to various domestic and international nonprofit groups.

We had our work cut out for us. What were we to become? How were we to build an endowment? What would be our first steps? Who might help us along the way? The first thing I did was talk with Dad about how we could become a more strategically driven organization, combining his '60s idealism with my '90s practicality, while leading with the same heart! We began to build an endowment, recruit an active governing board, and meet with a variety of colleagues from the music industry for a series of planning and visioning exercises.

All the while, I was continuing to grow my own business. My husband and I moved out of New York City to rural Vermont and our second child was born. Life was busy.

Now ten years later, PDF has most of its questions answered, having evolved into a foundation that supports and furthers music for social change. Our programs include a biannual songwriting contest and concert for music of social and political conscience. We are working to develop an interactive online portal where people can see how artists (both celebrities and lesser known) are making a difference through their music and activism. And of course, we still give money to worthy nonprofits each year (one of my favorite things to do). With the work we've accomplished thus far, and the encouragement we've gotten from various musicians, both known and aspiring, the organization could become *the source* for music that inspires social change, serves as a catalyst for social justice movements and generates educational messages about the issues of our day.

Although given the title and role of Executive Director, I am essentially still operating as a volunteer, struggling to do this all in my spare time. At a recent strategic planning meeting, the current board questioned whether my level of 'volunteerism' is now appropriate. They all agree that I'm doing a great job, but at what point should a highly active volunteer become a paid employee so the organization's goals can be fully realized? And what about me: am I ready and willing to take on this role as a job?

These new questions make me realize something about my volunteering philosophy (perhaps it may resonate with others). When you are a volunteer, you can make significant contributions and your accomplishments seem magnified because you are not a paid staff person. Similarly, any mistakes you make seem less significant, as in, "Well, she's only a volunteer, doing this in her spare time, what can we really expect?" But what happens when you begin to earn money for a labor of love? Do perceptions of you and your work change? Do people's expectations of your output rise? Does the possibility of failure become more intense? In short, yes! But if you are continuing to follow your heart, and you are doing the good work you did as a dedicated volunteer, then I have to think that marvelous things can happen.

So what will I do? And, once again, do I really have a choice? This time I have a chance to take volunteering a step further, uniting my need to make a living with my desire to make a difference in the world. Here I am, once again crossing Dad's vocational path with my passion for social change—leading with my head, guided by my heart, in concert with my father...and without ever having learned to play guitar!

 For more information about Public Domain Foundation, or to purchase the "Wedding Song" gift package/favor that benefits charities worldwide, visit www.pdfoundation.org.

Twelve Minute Cab Ride

BY NIPUN MEHTA

"Penn Station," I told the cab driver. The young, heavy-set man peered at me through his sunglasses and motioned for me to get in.

"I've got to get to JFK airport by 2:30 p.m. You think I'll be able to get there via LIRR or should I cab it all the way?" I asked him, as I got comfortable in the back seat.

"Hmmm. You should be okay. Yeah, you'll make it. It will be much cheaper to take the train," he replied in a mild South Asian accent.

"Thanks," I told him. Given his engaging nature, we naturally started a conversation, which quickly veered from the weather to the struggles of a cab driver's life. "How long have you been driving cabs?" "Three years." "You like it?" "It's really hard work. Not all people are so nice. I get tired, but what can you do? You have to pay the bills." "I hear you."

Like most New York cab drivers, he accelerated constantly and braked often, zoomed through red lights, almost nicked a couple of cars and still, never broke a sweat.

"What do you do?" he asked curiously.

"I help a nonprofit organization trying to bring some goodness to the world," I responded.

"Do they pay you well?"

"Well, no but I get by. I don't have many material things. The IRS would consider me poor, but you know, I don't need all that much to keep me happy. If I die tomorrow, I want to go out knowing that I've made a few people smile."

The young cab driver, perhaps in his late thirties, looked back through the sliding glass as if extending his hand for a handshake— "Man, it is nice to meet you," he said. "It is really nice to meet you." Although we were strangers, both of us felt deeply connected as human beings. And by now, seven minutes into our ride, we were on a first-name basis. He even spelled his name for me: H-a-k-e-e-m.

Hakeem and I talked a bit about simple acts of generosity, the power of a pay-it-forward mindset and how that can promote trust and connection in our communities. These ideas seemed very abstract and foreign to him, so I gave him the example of a restaurant in Berkeley called "Karma Kitchen."

"So, you walk into this restaurant and you get a meal without paying for it. Your bill says $0.00 because someone before you has paid for your meal. Then, if you want, you pay-forward for the person after you. You pay whatever you want for someone you don't even know."

"So do the homeless go to this restaurant?" Hakeem asked, confused.

"It's not like a soup-kitchen," I explained, "It's a place where everyone comes in."

"Wow, really? That is something," he pondered aloud.

Our conversation was one of those lively, happy conversations. We were both laughing it up and sharing stories, when he turned to me and said, "Can I keep in touch with you? I want to help. I want to be associated with this." Perhaps it broke protocol for a cab driver to ask for the business card of a customer, but Hakeem and I felt like old friends. "Sure thing, buddy," I replied. We traded email addresses as he informed me that he has a laptop at home from which he can check emails once every couple of days.

"You know what you could do, Hakeem?" I suggested in a conspiring tone. "You could give free rides to people every so often, and see how they respond. Imagine the dinner conversation that they would have with their family that night."

"Wow. Yeah. I will do that. Every week, I can give away a $5 cab ride." After a reflective pause, he added, "Man, I'm moved."

We arrived at Penn Station. The total was $14.15. I gave him $15 and was looking through my wallet for more when he immediately planted a dollar bill into my hands and insisted that I not tip him— "No, no. Please, please." It was 15 cents from a cabbie, but in his heart, Hakeem was giving me a free ride and I was blessed to receive it.

As I was headed out, I turned to him and said, "Hakeem, you know how we talked about this pay-it-forward idea? Well, here's a $20 bill. Whenever you feel like it, give a ride to people and tell them that someone before them has paid for their fare. See what happens." Hearing this, Hakeem was visibly moved.

"Really? Are you sure?"

"Absolutely."

"I will give them your email address too."

"No, no. This is not about you or me. Ask them to just pay-it-forward. And here, give them a Smile Card," I said as I handed him a couple of cards that encourage people to keep the ripple of kindness flowing.

Standing on the streets, I looked in through the back window and said, "Alright, my friend, be well." Almost speechless, he repeated one last time: "Man, I'm moved." So was I.

Nipun Mehta is the founder of CharityFocus, a fully volunteer-run organization that leverages technology to inspire greater volunteerism and shift our cultural ethos towards generosity. Visit www.charityfocus.org and www.helpothers.org to read more stories of kindness and to find out about the Karma Kitchen, Smile Cards and more.

Legislative Birdwatchers

BY JOAN REINHARDT REISS

As a skilled organic chemist with a Master's degree and many years of experience, my heart yearned for a Ph.D. In 1965, my husband Mark, a diagnostic radiologist, was hired by a Baltimore hospital and I was accepted in the biochemistry department at John Hopkins Medical School. With two toddlers, we moved to the suburbs. The biochemistry world was a male bastion with few females and no mothers. Rigorous science classes had graduate students competing against medical students while I struggled between children and academia.

The written exams required to enter the Ph.D. research world were intense. I failed; a Ph.D. dream ended. In my devastated state, a professor met with me. To insure my permanent exit from science, he said, "Just go home and take care of your children."

A year later, we returned to California where Mark joined a large Sacramento radiology group. In the early 60s, we'd spent three delicious years in Palo Alto during Mark's Stanford residency. I held a high-powered research position with Syntex, a pharmaceutical company known for the birth control pill. Nobel Prize winners came to brown bag lunches to review our work.

When Mark received the invitation to join the Sacramento radiology group, we celebrated our California return with warm champagne and hugs. But Mark cautioned, "Just remember Joan, Sacramento isn't Palo Alto."

Sacramento, capitol of the Golden State—often called "Cow

Town" or "Tomato Capital"—was boiling hot in the summer and foggy in the winter. However, beckoning nearby was the biochemistry department at the University of California at Davis where I might have another chance at a Ph.D. Unfortunately, the Chairman knew both my Hopkins professor and my old problems. I explained that I now had solid childcare and a fellowship was unnecessary. He said, "If you take two years of undergraduate science, I'll be happy to review your grades and decide if you're graduate material." What an insult! I couldn't possibly revisit the undergraduate world. I realized my Ph.D. desire would be unfulfilled indefinitely.

When Earth Day arrived in 1970, I decided if I couldn't get the degree I wanted, I would join the Sierra Club and save the world. I barely understood my intentions, but this decision was to change my life forever.

The Sacramento Sierra Club was committed to supporting environmental legislation, but a huge problem existed. The California legislature consists of two houses: Assembly and Senate. When an entire house votes on a bill, it is called a "floor vote." With a floor vote, each vote is recorded, printed, and easily obtained by the public. However, votes in the smaller legislative committees were never recorded. A few casual "Ayes" and some mumbled "Nays" meant that the committee Chairman often killed good laws before they had a chance. Those responsible for the "Nays" were anonymous.

So a Sierra Club colleague and I founded the all-volunteer corps to attend committees and record the votes on environmental issues. Our small but energetic group was comprised of high school students, senior citizens, teachers, and committed conservationists. We called ourselves "the Legislative Birdwatchers." For easy recognition, we wore tags with yellow canary-like birds and a tree in the center. Thus armed for battle, we attended committee sessions to record votes on key environmental bills. We observed that there were devious ways to vote: a stealthy note to the chairman, finger movement up or down, and the ubiquitous mutter. Votes were difficult to decipher—but we tried. Two or even three Birdwatchers went to each committee hearing. In order to validate a legislator's vote, we phoned his office and asked, "In committee today, Senator Smith voted on Senate bill 385. Could you tell me how he voted?" Common responses were: "He never tells me that" and "I have no idea."

When the legislative session ended, we had a dishearteningly small amount of data but an overactive publicist. Our thin photo-copied report began, "Who Murdered the Environment? Now the killers can be known!" Overnight we were a media sensation. Along with making some legislators disgruntled, we also upset the Sacramento Audubon Society, a rather apolitical organization. I appeared before the Executive Board and was accused of bird watching blasphemy! The Audubon Society demanded an immediate name change. I pleaded with them, "Please understand, we have media attention, a recognized name, and a need to continue shining light on environmental committee votes. We just can't remove Birdwatchers from our name." These details did not mollify the unhappy Audubon board. Nevertheless, our environmental vote counts continued as did our reports.

As the 1972 legislative session began, we had an unexpected champion: Senator Peter Behr, an urbane, elegant Republican from Marin County. His district began north of San Francisco, across the Golden Gate Bridge. As a leader of many environmental causes, he was influential in the creation of the Point Reyes National Seashore. When Peter Behr introduced legislation to record all committee votes, several of his less honorable colleagues mocked him for capitulating to those pesky Birdwatchers. But the bill passed, and the *Sacramento Bee* newspaper wrote that "the people of California should be forever grateful to the Legislative Birdwatchers for recorded committee votes." Personally, I was hooked onto a career as an environmental policy advocate.

Now after 38 years as a public policy advocate for the environment and environmental health, I am a writer, occasional commentator on public radio, and grandmother (aka Bubba). True I failed a Ph.D. exam; but I'm leaving the state of California just a tiny bit better than it might have been had my original scholarly plan worked out. Life is so good. I am committed to enjoying it and protecting it. After all, with a 49 year marriage to the same person, I am an endangered species myself!

Joan Reinhardt Reiss is a freelance writer and commentary contributor to San Francisco's KQED public radio. She is also an environmental health consultant, primarily serving the Breast Cancer Fund, the only national nonprofit whose sole focus is to identify—and advocate for elimination of—environmental causes of the disease.

Kids Helping Kids

BY LAURA PAGE

In spite of a spirit of volunteerism that many of us share, we have been guilty of over-indulging our children and not educating them about the dark realities beyond our Western civilization.

All that is changing in my family. My ten-year-old son, Tyler, has become an agent for change by imagining, planning, and implementing a project that is impacting the world.

Tyler is a year older than his brother Ryan and the two of them are great friends. Tyler was always the more self-absorbed of the two. He would do such things as accidentally slam into a toddler at the bottom of a slide, then go on his way, unaware that the toddler left behind was crying. He was an egocentric child who would get grumpy if he didn't get what he wanted to eat or if he couldn't watch the movie he wanted to watch. He also had an Alpha personality and would make up games with his own set of rules and tell his friends how to play.

Everything changed last year when Tyler was in the fourth grade. He came into my room while I was watching a show on Oprah called, "The Little Boy Oprah Couldn't Forget." The show was about parents in Ghana who would sell their young children to traders for as little as $20.

After the show, Tyler asked me many questions about human trafficking. When I would try to explain, he would get upset and say "Stop it!" But then he'd bring it up again.

Finally Tyler said, "Can we do a fundraiser and then send the money to Oprah to help one of these children?"

"How would you do it?" I asked.

"I would tell my classmates about it; see if they would like to help."

He ended up writing a letter to his classmates and they organized a car wash. When people called out of their cars to ask who they were doing the car wash for, they shouted back, "For kids with nothing!"

Tyler's goal was to get $240 to rescue one child, but in two weeks they raised $1,100—enough for 4.7 children according to Oprah's figure. The next day in church I shared our story, explaining how we needed just $70 more for that fifth child. Afterwards one of the parishioners handed me an envelope that he said was for the fifth child, but the envelope actually contained a check for $500!

This unexpected contribution encouraged Tyler to reset his goals. When he asked my advice I told him, "Reach for the stars. You never know how much you can get." He began organizing more car washes and lemonade sales with an aim to raise $50,000 before the end of the year. Little brother Ryan became a great supporter. He attends all the events, cheerfully performing such tasks as handing out cookies and dishing up ice cream.

I've become a specialist on Project Ghana. With Tyler's vision, I started an organization named Kids Helping Kids. We recently received our nonprofit status. Through Kids Helping Kids, we're extending our outreach, utilizing ideas and efforts from other kids and their families. This Christmas we sent 500 backpacks full of school supplies to rescued children and over 6,000 bags of treats to our troops.

For me, one of the most wonderful things that has occurred though this series of events is the positive change in Tyler. From increased patience to a greater awareness of those around him, he is now more mature than his years.

We recently attended a baseball game where Tyler saw a little girl sitting by herself while three other kids played nearby. Tyler stopped his scooter and said to the girl, "Hi! What's your name? My name is Tyler. You don't look very happy." Immediately the girl brightened and started talking with him. Then he took her over to the other kids and they all started playing together.

When we were leaving the park Tyler explained, "I helped the girls work through a fight. It turned out that one of them was lying, but I helped them work it out."

Amazing! This is a 180° reversal from the boy I used to know. Tyler noticed the little girl had a problem, and more importantly, he investigated the problem and then implemented a solution. That's the kind of human being he is becoming. He now believes he can make a difference and extends himself to do so. And his Alpha personality is being put to good use as he leads his peers in good causes.

Our new organization, Kids Helping Kids, is not just about assisting needy children in other countries. It's also about listening to our *own* children and mobilizing them to respond to the greater needs of the world.

The original version of this article first appeared in *110°*, January/February. 2008. For more information on Kids Helping Kids, go to www.kidzhelpingkids.com.

Life at the Kettle: Fourteen Days
As a Salvation Army Bell Ringer

BY THE REV. BETH ERNEST

Geographical moves might be considered the biggest test of compromise in the modern marriage. In the spring of 2003, my husband was offered a position at a publishing house in Grand Rapids, Michigan. For him it was a good opportunity, and I had just finished an interim pastorate, so we loaded up two cars, two kids, fifty cartons of books, and all our other earthly possessions and headed west from New England to our new home.

As James settled in to a new routine and the kids became involved with a new ballet school, a new violin teacher, and new friends, I was left to unpack and chauffeur offspring. Despite activity, I was unprepared for the great void that came to my life. I had pastored five churches in New Hampshire, and my heart beat to the ebb and flow of parish life. An unfulfilled longing for my pastoral calling frustrated me in ways my family could not understand. Sometimes I had to leave worship services (planned by others with no help from me!) because I could not suppress tears of grief. My pastor's ears were alert to counseling opportunities among people who neither wanted nor asked for my services. Had God's call to me been revoked? It was a sadness I could not bear.

Continued unemployment was not an option as months passed and the family coffers felt the squeeze. But who would hire an unemployed pastor? Ministry opportunities did not work out due to wrong timing or "wrong" gender or "wrong" denominational affiliation. I decided to try the secular route. An import-export firm declared me overeducated. A sewing store pointed out my lack of cash register skills.

A sweep of the want ads in November revealed an opening almost anyone could fill—the Salvation Army needed bell ringers. Résumé in hand, I went to the largest citadel, only to be denied! I would have to agree to be transported to my assigned location by a Salvation Army van leaving from a difficult location at an impossible hour. Discouraged, I headed to a smaller unit. There, a kindly officer took interest in my plight. Of course I could help. Of course I could drive myself. He would even keep his eyes open for other ministry opportunities for me. Thank you, God!

I was prepared to accept snow and cold for hours on end. I was willing (by that time, delighted) to accept twenty-five cents over minimum wage. What was going to be hard for me was the very symbol of the job itself—the incessantly ringing, monotonous, tinny bell. Going out on a limb with my new employer, I asked if I might be excused from ringing the bell. Instead, I would sing!

"Can you sing?" he asked. After I assured him that I had paid good money to learn to sing, he dubiously recounted the tale of a woman who had likewise insisted on singing and had gone on to offend the ears of everyone at her location outside a drug store. But just short of an impromptu audition, he smiled and agreed that I should sing, ringing the bell only when my voice needed a rest. My location was to be a local Target store with an overhang that would, he said, act as a good acoustical backdrop for music! At last, a job I could do.

Back on the home front, my husband was bemused at my new-found purpose. I woke the first morning of my new position, wrapped myself in layers of wool, loaded up *The Oxford Book of Carols* and my Messiah score, and headed to my very own kettle at Target. Since I worked the first shift, a Salvation Army van arrived shortly after my arrival bringing the accoutrements of the Bell Ringer: a bell, an apron, an official nametag, and a ruler. Seeing that the ruler puzzled me, the driver explained that a Bell Ringer is never allowed to touch the money. The giver must put the money in the slot on the kettle. If it doesn't go down, the ruler is used to stuff the money in, thus keeping the Bell Ringer free from suspicion of theft.

It is hard to explain how exhilarating that first day was. Stupidly, I had not warmed up adequately and did feel the effect of singing off and on for six hours! That aside, I was unprepared for what I experienced. I thought I had signed up to help the Salvation Army raise money. What I found instead was that I had signed up to proclaim the good news of the Christmas story again and again through the words of the ancient carols.

We are used to singing just a few verses of a few carols around the Christmas season, but my time at the kettle with the larger repertoire revealed a theological depth in these beautiful songs I had not noticed before. Take, for instance, a timely verse usually left out of *It Came upon a Midnight Clear* by Edmund Sears:

> Yet with the woes of sin and strife
> The world has suffered long;
> Beneath the angel strain have rolled
> Two thousand years of wrong;
> And man, at war with man, hears not
> The love-song which they bring;
> O hush the noise, ye men of strife
> And hear the angels sing.

Or words of wisdom from a Sussex folk carol:

> When sin departs before his grace,
> Then life and health come in its place:
> Angels and men with joy may sing
> All for to see their newborn king!

For the next two weeks I was touched not only by the carols from many centuries and cultures, but the effect this music had on the shoppers. Countless people thanked me for singing carols ("We don't hear the carols any more"). Dozens of parents stopped so their children could listen ("They don't learn carols in school any more"). The kettle was a natural for stewardship lessons, parents beaming as children's little hands dropped money into the slot. I asked these young givers if they knew where the money went and we talked about the poor children their generosity would serve.

Often people asked for requests or asked to sing along. One man hobbled up to the kettle and said bluntly, "I want to sing one with you. One is all I can do. How about 'Joy to the World'?" I asked him to pitch it for his voice and he let loose with a deep, sweet baritone that floated over the parking lot. After we finished, he said he had not celebrated Christmas in twelve years and thanked me profusely for allowing him to have Christmas again. Another day, three college girls came forward giggling, as if on a dare. They sang a delightfully off-pitch verse of "Silent Night" before giggling their way into the store to shop till they dropped.

Cups of coffee and hot chocolate appeared from shoppers leaving the store, deposited with a smile atop my song books. A security officer paid for my lunch before I could pay the cashier. Another employee frequently stopped by to discuss her recent diagnosis and talk about the Dutch carols her father had sung. I prayed for her. A smartly dressed woman came up and stuffed a large bill into the kettle. Leaning in close, she said, "Thank you! If it weren't for the Salvation Army, I wouldn't have had Christmas as a child."

Singing at the kettle gave the opportunity to reach a wide audience with God's Word. These were not all people who would self-select to attend a church service. They were not all people who necessarily believe that "Mary bore sweet Jesus Christ for to redeem us all." Nevertheless they could hear the story of Love that came to earth and participate in the generosity his love awakens.

The financial gain from two weeks at twenty-five cents over minimum wage was lowly indeed. The real blessing came in the humbling opportunity to proclaim words of Truth from a kettle pulpit, words sung by countless faithful voices throughout the ages. There was the welcome assurance to my uprooted soul that God's call is not only for those times when we sit at trustee meetings and hold positions of leadership. Rather, throughout fourteen glorious days, God reminded me that his call is irrevocable, and it belongs to him, not to me.

> O Holy Child of Bethlehem,
> Descend to us, we pray;
> Cast out our sin and enter in;
> Be born in us today!
> We hear the Christmas angels
> The great glad tidings tell;
> O come to us, abide with us,
> Our Lord Emmanuel!

Beth Ernest is a pastor in the Evangelical Covenant Church, currently serving Dowagiac Covenant Church as Interim Pastor. She lives in Caledonia, MI, with her husband, two teenagers, and an Irish Terrier. She has pastored churches in New Hampshire and served as a hospice chaplain. This article was first published in *The Covenant Companion*, Dec. 2007.

Kenny

BY CHRIS MALCOMB

When I tell people that I spent a year as a volunteer English teacher in the college program at San Quentin State Prison they often wonder if I ever felt afraid. I answer this question very carefully. In a place as complicated as San Quentin, reality can become distorted by assumptions.

I cannot describe the "typical" San Quentin student. Despite some external similarities—the ubiquitous blue clothing; the standard yellow mesh bags; the hardened, self-protective gaze—the men I met came from vastly divergent lifestyles and backgrounds. They spanned the spectrum of age, race, and educational experience. Some were cheerful and chatty; others were moody and unpredictable. I met men who practiced yoga and meditation, attended AA meetings, and played on the prison baseball or soccer teams. Some were writing film scripts and novels. Many believed in God. Others didn't. Several didn't think it even mattered. Incarcerated for all manner of crimes, some anxiously awaited the end of their term or an upcoming parole hearing, while others were well into life sentences.

Like any teacher, I was inspired when tapped into the fiercely intellectual sides of my students, stimulated by their hunger for attention, challenge, and growth. I loved seeing one finally grasp the structure of a good paragraph, craft a strong thesis, or more deeply understand an author's use of setting or theme. Instances like these energized me, and while I dedicated hours to providing individualized feedback to ensure their continuance, I most enjoyed stepping aside as my students soared forward. In fact, I cannot recall a teaching experience in which my "self" disappeared so completely. Inside the prison my entire focus was to serve.

Yet there was another side. While proud to contribute to such a vibrant, forward-moving community, I sometimes felt confused by the paradox of the men's lives. The first student I ever met was a handsome, clean-cut African-American man in his mid-50s. He wore wire-rimmed glasses, and carried a stack of books including Calculus I and Albert Camus' *The Stranger*. Had I met him elsewhere I might have assumed he was a literature professor or a psychiatrist, but here I had to grapple with the fact that this soft-spoken, poetic man was also a convicted felon. I would teach many others like him—men whose charm and intellect completely conflicted with my image of convicts—as well as those who, with lives marked by poverty, poor education, drugs, or gang activity, did reinforce such stereotypes, at least on the surface. I had never considered that my experience would both confirm and challenge what I thought I knew about people living behind bars.

Early in my second semester I attended a talk by Bo Lozof, founder of The Prison Ashram Project. "Imagine being known for the worst thing you ever did in your life," he said, speaking about the burden of incarceration. "This is your defining label. Everywhere you go. Forever. Imagine that." Lozof's words helped me understand that even as my mind questioned what was "true" about the men in my classroom, I needed to avoid the temptation of concrete labels and focus on what I was there to do: teach. The curriculum could be a neutral zone, a safe meeting point between two worlds.

Despite this effort, I struggled. As inspiring as my best students were, others tested the limits of my knowledge and patience. Some challenged my every critique. Some skipped assignments, failed to revise work, or simply lacked the skill for college-level writing. Many just stopped coming to class. Although I knew that letting students skip discussions or write papers with weak thesis statements and no supporting evidence was complacent—perhaps even damaging—it was certainly tempting.

In addition, asking my students to reach beyond their own fixed images of themselves—to *believe* that they could achieve and succeed—also forced me to examine my own preconceptions. I was shocked to realize that in difficult situations I *did* view some men as less capable, and that my judgments sometimes grew from unfounded perceptions about their age, race, personality, or background. It was amazing to observe how quickly such thoughts clouded my entire view of a student and while I generally let them pass without influencing my actions, one night I danced closer than ever to this fragile line.

I met Kenny during my second semester. His eyes were like glacial ice, shimmering blue and nearly transparent. He possessed an angular, rigid body, with greased-back brown hair, a bushy mustache, and lean arms lathered in tattoos of skulls, vines, bleeding hearts, and naked women. Sometimes Kenny entered class appearing slightly over-caffeinated—eyes darting, body twitching; sometimes he seemed sedated.

Despite possessing strong concrete thinking and recall skills, Kenny frequently struggled to formulate complex concepts. When discouraged, he slouched, exhaled forcefully, or made loud, unrelated statements in the middle of class discussions. When talking about his own work, he sometimes exhibited a curious measure of self-protection, disguising his deficiencies in a manic blur of false bravado. The nights when Kenny strutted into class announcing that he'd "nailed" an assignment were those during which I proceeded with great caution. I always began with positive feedback about obvious successes: proper spelling and grammar, clear paragraph structure, strong topic sentences. Only then could I hint at necessary revisions.

One night Kenny bounded into class grinning and waving three crumpled, smudged pages in the air. His eyes sparkled as he sat at his heavy oak desk and dropped his yellow mesh bag on the cold, cracked cement floor. "Got a good one, Chris," he said as he pushed his legs forward. The desk's metal feet screeched. He was talking about the rough draft of his essay about Charlotte Perkins-Gilman's "The Yellow Wallpaper," a story in which a husband commits his wife to extended bed-rest to "cure" her depression. As a result of her confinement to the top floor, the wife descends into madness.

I slid into the desk next to Kenny and took his draft. He slouched slightly, gazing downward and tapping his pencil nervously as I read. When I'd finished, he pursed his lips and shifted his eyes towards me. I pictured similar scenes. Kenny's teachers. Kenny's parents. Kenny's friends. I wondered how many times he had been criticized. His anxiety seeped through his skin like sweat.

So did mine.

"It's a strong theory," I said.

"Really?" he said.

I nodded. Yes. It was one we'd discussed in class: the husband was imprisoning his wife. The theory was good, and provable. The fact that Kenny's essay didn't prove it, however, would have to wait. I nodded and tapped the draft with my finger. "And you've done some really great things."

Kenny rose slightly in his seat. "Like what?" he said, sort of disbelieving.

I made a list. Clear introduction. Some good topic sentences. A thorough summary of the story, and relatively few spelling errors. And, I added with emphasis while trying to avoid patronizing, he had demonstrated a keen eye for the *details,* clearly describing specifics of the woman's room and the intricacies of the yellow wallpaper. "It's those concrete skills," I said, "that will help you make the next step."

Perhaps Kenny was in a trusting mood. Maybe he wanted the challenge that night, or thought my suggestions would be minimal. Either way, he opened a small window for constructive feedback. I slipped through carefully. His eyes remained wide and friendly as I explained how analytical thinkers learn to see *between* the words. "What seems a simple story about a woman locked in a bedroom may *actually* be much more," I said excitedly.

Suddenly his energy shifted. He slid his desk back a fraction of an inch. He squinted, and furrowed his brow. He tapped his pencil more forcefully.

He didn't get it.

Worried he might get frustrated—or even angry—I exhaled and quickly changed tactics. "OK. Let's talk about adjectives. Can you *describe* the husband?"

He buoyed slightly. This he understood. "Controlling. Possessive."

"I agree," I said. "Now, it's one thing to *say* he's possessive. But it's entirely different to *show* that." I explained that he could use the details he'd already recalled so well—the color and texture of the wallpaper, the furniture in the house, the characters' interactions—as evidence to support his theory. "Do any of those things show the husband's possessiveness?"

Kenny thumbed his dog-eared story, littered with stains, highlights, underlining, and scribbled marginalia. "Well…" he said. "The windows have bars on them."

"Great. A very clear image." I pushed further. "And if you really think about it…could the bars on those windows stand for anything?"

"Uh…" he said, stammering slightly. He shrugged his shoulders and exhaled. His breath smelled like old coffee and cigarettes. He looked stumped.

"Are those bars *protecting* her?"

"Yeah!" he said. "Maybe her husband's afraid that she's gonna jump out the window. He knows she's going crazy."

I kept my opinion to myself. "OK, protection. That's a possibility. Anything else?" I glanced around, noting the thick metal mesh and iron bars covering our windows. The room suddenly felt smaller, more confined.

Kenny straightened further, confidently. "Trapped? Yeah…the bars are like a cage. She's trapped in the room."

"And who's doing that?"

"She stays up there. She could get up and leave at any time."

"Really?"

Kenny riffled through his story again. His eyes buzzed the text. He was intent, focused. He found a page, fished a yellow highlighter from his bag, and began illuminating words. "OK, not really. It's her husband that keeps her there. He even locks the door."

This was exciting. I smiled. "What else?"

"The bed," he said. "It's nailed to the floor. And there are rings in the walls, like in a dungeon." He slapped his desk lightly and leaned back, raising his arms above his head. "Shit, it *is* just like in a prison. She's being held captive. By her husband!" He looked up, his eyes shining like tiny kaleidoscopes.

I told Kenny he should write his examples down. He did. Satisfied that he was on his way, I left to engage other men in similar conversations—honing theories, finding evidence, constructing clear, authoritative paragraphs. Periodically I glanced at him. His focus was uneven: sometimes he was writing or reading; sometimes he was laughing with a classmate or playing with his pencil. I thought about checking in, but hadn't yet reached everyone needing feedback. Plus, I'd already spent nearly a half-hour with him. After awhile I forgot about him entirely. I was discussing concluding paragraphs with Marius when the bell rang. The men began packing and putting on their coats.

"OK," I said to the group. "Finished drafts are due next class." I turned to say a last word to Marius when I heard a loud crash across the room.

BANG!

"How the FUCK…"

BANG!

A surge of adrenaline pulsed through my body. I turned. Kenny's face was flushed. He had kicked his desk to the wall. "How the fuck are we supposed to get them done if we can't get any help?" He slammed his materials into his bag. His pencil fell to the floor. He didn't pick it up.

Several men stopped. Others packed and left as if nothing was amiss. Kenny continued mumbling under his breath. I looked around. The men that remained in the room were waiting for my reaction. I swallowed, my throat suddenly parched.

Then the images came.

I couldn't stop them. They surged into my mind with blinding force. The more I resisted, the more they pounded. In a microsecond my conditioned, fearful mind had rendered Kenny unrecognizable: a caricature, a stereotype, a frightening stranger. Suddenly I was gazing not at a student, but a criminal. I imagined Kenny's crime. Did he joyride someone's car before torching it? Did he assault an old man? Was he a rapist? The images validated my fear, widening the fracture now placing us on the opposite sides of innocence.

It got worse. In a matter of seconds, I had transformed Kenny into someone who could commit—who *had* committed—murder. I knew it. Kenny had killed someone. Someone who had made him angry. In a situation like this. I shivered at the unfair thought. I didn't even know Kenny. I hadn't seen his file, or asked him about his life before prison. Still, I couldn't escape it. Murderer! What was I doing here? What would I do now?

In the years since that moment I've realized that Kenny, if like most incarcerated men, had simply never had a safe, nonjudgmental place to release his accumulated tension. Even if neither of us knew it, his outburst was much like a little boy throwing a temper tantrum. It was both a cry for attention and a test. Would I honor his feelings and give him space to be angry? Would I counter his aggression with my own? Or would I simply slip away in fear and never come back? I don't recall making a calculated decision, but deep inside I must have sensed that my response to Kenny's aggression would be equally—if not more—important as our conversation about "The Yellow Wallpaper." And so I walked across the room on wobbly legs, directly to where he was standing. I pulled his desk back into the circle, took a deep breath, and sat down.

"What's up Kenny?" I said, my voice cracking slightly.

He looked down at me, his eyes now lasers. "Been raisin' my *freakin'* hand for an hour. You *told* me to work on those examples. I did, and you disappeared." He squeezed his bag. His fingers were white, his body stiff like a spool of wire. He continued through clenched teeth. "Haven't had *shit* to do since cause I need to know if I got it right."

"Oh man," I said with a sigh, gripping the edge of the desk. It was a lie. He *hadn't* been trying to get my attention. He *hadn't* raised his hand. He *hadn't* said a word. Not for a whole hour. We both knew it. "I'm so sorry I missed your hand."

"Well…it don't matter now," he said. Beads of sweat trickled down his forehead.

"I guess I got too wrapped up in moving around the room," I said.

Kenny continued packing. He flexed his fists. He stared at the floor. "Ain't no time left now. Bell's rang. Don't know how you expect me to finish this paper. Can't even find out if I'm doing it right." He looked at me once more, moving closer. I felt the heat coming off his body. I arched back slightly. "Thanks a *lot,*" he said. He threw his bag over his shoulder and stormed out of the room.

I remained seated. Shaking. Breathing in short, shallow bursts. Several of the men turned and left. Tears started to form in my eyes. Fear? Relief? I gingerly assembled my materials and reached for my jacket. Sadness?

Marius approached. "Don't be trippin', Chris," he said. "Kenny's just like that. He'll cool off." He extended his hand. "Thanks for your help tonight."

I returned the handshake. Marius' grip was thick and muscular. My knuckles cracked as he squeezed. After he left, I sat perfectly still for several minutes. The classroom was empty. The lights buzzed, and voices echoed beyond the mesh-covered windows. The men were returning to their cells. As I stood up I noticed that Kenny's pencil was still on floor. The tip was broken. I set it in the box containing our supplies, and walked upstairs to the storage locker, stopping at a pencil sharpener along the way.

The following week, I showed up for class as usual. Kenny smiled as he handed me his paper. "Got a good one, Chris," he said. His eyes were bright and happy. I gave him his pencil. Neither of us said a word about what had happened.

The Prison University Project can be researched at www.prisonuniversityproject.org. Chris Malcomb is an MFA student at the University of San Francisco and teaches writing to both kids and adults. His work has appeared in *San Francisco Chronicle Magazine, Narrative.com, Grassroots Fundraising Journal,* and *Teachers & Writers.* He practices meditation, drinks looseleaf Chinese tea, and can be reached at cwmalcomb@hotmail.com

When Consumerism Calls

BY MICHELE SBRANA

I have once again emerged from the abyss that regularly and mercilessly swallows unsuspecting women like me, draining them of energy, judgment and money before spitting them back out as heavy-laden shells of their former selves. I'm talking about Target. What is it about that place? Is there a spell cast upon me as I pass through those red, electronic sliding doors? ("Mich-shhhh-ele," they sweetly whisper as they open, and again, "Mich-shhhh-ele," as they close.)

I dutifully compose a shopping list in the Target parking lot, on the back of what is probably a very important receipt (which I found crumpled beneath my brake pedal), and promise myself that I will adhere to it absolutely: tennis balls, brown lunch bags and goldfish crackers. I clutch the list tightly and keep it within eyesight as I grab my crimson cart. But as God is my witness, once inside the vastness that is Target, with its endless aisles stocked with every consumer good that any consumer in the history of consumerism has ever consumed, I am powerless to resist. My otherwise discerning mind begins to utter these words the moment I breathe the rarefied air of the Target vestibule, with its giant red bulls-eye that should more aptly be painted on my back than on their wall: I need, I want, I must have…

I *need* the twelve-ply, double-roll, twenty-four pack of toilet paper…I *need* that thirty-seven liter jug of laundry detergent…I *must have* that cleverly antiqued garden sign and matching garden hose spigot…my kids *want* those Scooby Doo electric toothbrushes…my husband *needs* those seersucker Bermuda shorts. Before I know it, I've topped off my cart with a talking cookie jar, a case of cinnamon toaster strudel and four pairs of summer flip-flops (because last year's flip-flops are just so *last year*). The original list with the tennis balls, brown lunch bags and goldfish crackers has gotten buried somewhere beneath the new doormat for Halloween, a lifetime supply of cotton balls (because we used up our last lifetime supply), and a couple of bottles of my favorite chardonnay…because who doesn't need a drink after such an exhausting day?

I might be exaggerating ever so slightly, but honestly, I've long been embarrassed by my chronic lack of self-control in that place. Lately, however, the real source of my shopping angst has changed. For lack of a better way of putting it, I've grown a shopping conscience. Part of it comes from simply wanting my kids to learn how to appreciate what they do have rather than whine about what they don't. And as much as I hate to admit it, contentment is a trickle-down attitude. They need to see me asking myself, "Do I really need…the cookie jar, the door mat, the flip-flops…?" Recently I taped a note to my bathroom mirror that reads "Be a consumer of only what you need today." It helps.

But in addition to my parenting concerns, over the past several years I've had the chance to travel to a number of places in East Africa. I got to know people who live on less than $2 a day. I walked beside women who travel miles morning and evening to get water for their families. And I learned that a significant percentage of people in our world lives this way. Talk about a reality check.

And even more than that, I've seen people who actually suffer oppression because of the "stuff" that we citizens of wealthy nations insist on having at our disposal. For most of human history the majority of things people used or consumed were grown or built or created by themselves or someone they knew. We had "direct relationship" societies. But in today's post-industrialized society, few of us have any idea who made what we use, or where it really came from. We don't know who picked our strawberries or sewed the buttons on our blouses or bottled our milk or assembled our cell phones. And because we don't know, we often don't care.

But what if readily available goods at rock bottom prices means that someone somewhere is being exploited? Does it matter? I think it does. It matters who made my kids' shoes. Was she paid a decent wage? It matters where my coffee beans were picked. Are growers there treated fairly? It matters how the cotton for my pillowcases was harvested. Are the working conditions humane? I've come to understand that I really do have a relationship with the person who produces my goods. And even though that relationship is indirect, the fact is that if I'm drinking coffee harvested by someone who was exploited, in a way I'm participating in that exploitation.

As an American woman I have a lot of influence over the ways in which our family's money is spent. I've begun carrying a handy little shopping guide (*Better World Shopping Guide* by Ellis Jones) in my purse that rates products based on the way the company or corporation treats its employees and the surrounding environment. Sometimes it's really easy to switch from one product to another to support the company that is more honorable. Sometimes it means going without a product that I didn't really need anyway. Sometimes it means sending an email to a company and asking them to pay their employees a fair wage or make better environmental policies. A lot of the time it simply means shopping locally and knowing the people who make or grow the things you want.

I'm grateful that my shopping conscience is leading me to become a more compassionate consumer. And I look forward to the day when I'll drive out of the Target parking lot with nothing in the trunk but tennis balls, brown lunch bags and goldfish crackers.

Some of Michele's favorite social conscious shopping resources: AGreaterGift.org; BetterWorldShopper.com; Baksheesh (www.vom.com/baksheesh); DivineChocolate.com; GearThatGives.com; GroundsforChange.com; SweatShopWatch.org; TenThousandVillages.com; and TradeAsOne.org. To read more by Michele, go to www.michelesbrana.com.

"…a great door for effective work has opened to me…"
I Corinthians 16:8-9

The Open Door

BY LYNN TURNER

We first discovered the children as they played in the parking lot of the Peniel Mission where my husband Rich and I volunteered once a month, performing music with New Wine Creative Ministries. "Where do all these kids live?" we wondered. Then Millie Wong entered the scene.

A long-time supporter of the Mission, Millie spoke Cantonese and could communicate with the immigrants working at Chinese sweatshops hidden around the San Francisco Bay Area. She told us that the children came from one of these sweatshops, a nearby apartment complex owned and run by a woman who earned the title, "The Dragon Lady."

The Dragon Lady brought families over from Hong Kong with promises of a new life in America—that is, once they paid off their fees by working in her slave-like sewing business, eating at her restaurant and living in her one-room apartments. It could take years, if ever, for them to work their way out of bondage.

The children indebted to The Dragon Lady did not speak any English. They lacked warm clothes and didn't own a single toy as far as we could see. With Millie's help and translation ability, a few of us at the Mission decided to hold a Vacation Bible School. With cautious moms watching, a few kids attended the first day, but by the end of our outreach, over 70 needy immigrant and refugee kids came to have "fun"—a unique concept for them.

We contacted KTVU Channel 2, and they came out to do a

news piece on these "hidden children"—and we found hundreds of them! The cameramen were so touched by their plight, they came back the next day with donations of clothes and toys.

As our government continued to bring Southeast Asian refugees over from the camps in Thailand, the population grew. And Millie had a heart for them all. She would regularly do "her rounds," walking through the streets with a huge trunk full of clothes, food, and household goods to give away. Whenever she opened her trunk, refugees came flooding out of their apartments to receive her gifts. The need was amazing.

Occasionally, Rich and I went on the rounds with Millie, and we met people from Cambodia, Laos, and Vietnam—refugees who were just dumped into the inner city, knowing little about this country or how they would live here. I was shocked. They had no sponsors, no language and no cultural training. I found out later that 90% of these refugees were suffering deep depression from having seen their families slaughtered before their eyes and their ancestral lands of inheritance destroyed by a war they never chose. My heart broke over these people from "the killing fields."

Millie was in her late 60s and just couldn't continue all this mercy work by herself. We started to share her burden for the refugees—at times kicking and screaming. "But God, aren't we doing enough already?" I argued. We were volunteering at the Mission, performing with New Wine Creative Ministries, raising our own young children and, incidentally, we still had to earn money from our *real* jobs!

But this was clearly a "great door for an effective work," and it was wide open to me. As I gave myself to yet another service, I felt like I was being stretched to the max, but as soon as the tent pegs of my heart were moved further out, God's grace and love flooded in and gave me the strength to move forward.

Generous folks began to fill our very small suburban apartment with clothes, furniture, toys, and other useful items for the refugee families. We delivered the goods to them each Saturday. Some of our friends joined us and "adopted" families of their own to help. The need was so immense and overwhelming, we decided it would be best to limit ourselves to just one complex, which we dubbed "The Cambodian Village." Here 500 Khmer and Mienh lived like they were still in Cambodia and Laos. They kept their country's clothes, foods, customs and celebrations, and we were invited to experience them all—often resulting in social "bloopers." Once I walked over a large bamboo mat on the living room floor that just happened to be their dinner table. Once I intended to wish them a "good day" in Khmer, but I wished them a "good pillow" instead. Another time, I noticed several sealed brown bags in one of the corners of the room. The bags were moving and sometimes *jumping*! I tried not to say anything, but my curiosity got the better of me, so I asked what they were. They cheerfully answered, "Oh those are chickens. We will be having them for dinner! Can you stay?"

After ten years of serving my refugee friends, I have many more stories to tell. I so loved these people that I ended up living and teaching overseas, first in Cambodia and India and then in China and Nepal. Now back in the States, my American friends ask me, "How do you do all this—work in the Himalayas; start an orphanage with a High Priest of Bhutan; run a school in Pokhara; *and* open a restaurant with an ex-Tibetan monk who used to work with the Dalai Lama?"

"Well," I tell them, "It started with just one obedient step many years ago through an open door."

By the way, Millie, now 88 years old, tells me that she "didn't do much," but is amazed at how much good came from her small sacrifices of love for God and the refugees.

Lynn Turner serves as Overseer for the Himalayas for The Strategic Leadership Alliance, currently working with refugees from Tibet, Bhutan and North Korea. If you would like to volunteer to teach English, art or music or work in Kids Camps in China or Nepal, or help in medical clinics in Nepal, contact Lynn at: heart4thehimalayas@yahoo.com.

Voluntary Eating

BY LISA OTA

When it comes to volunteering our time and energy toward social causes, there is something all of us can do each and every day: eat! While we are required to eat in order to live, *what* and *how* we eat is, indeed, a voluntary act.

Food—its nutritional value and the pure delight of it—has always been of great interest to me. I can't think of anything more symbolic of our interconnectedness than food, the substance of life. No matter our gender, age, religion, social class, political affiliation, or ethnicity, we are all dependent upon food for life. Food demonstrates that, at our core, we are more similar to one another than we think.

Yet I've struggled to understand how something so fundamental to human existence has become fraught with so many problems. How did our nation become so addicted to one fad diet after another? How does it happen that so many people on our planet don't have enough to eat when the earth does, in fact, provide enough food for everyone? As a Registered Dietitian with degrees in Nutritional Sciences, Public Health Nutrition, and Creation Spirituality, my passion is to nurture our collective thinking on these issues.

Our society has become sadly desensitized to the origins of food; to what it takes to get food to our table. When we are at the grocery store, for example, we are unaware that the amount of water needed to make enough meat for one hamburger is equal to the amount of water used in one month by a family of four in the Amazon. Plus, for each pound of meat, our fields lose about five pounds of topsoil due to deforestation, overgrazing in areas too small to support the animal population, and the overuse of chemical fertilizers for crops used for animal feed. Further, it takes five to twenty calories of fossil fuel to produce one calorie of food energy in the form of meat. Far more energy-efficient is the production of plant food. There are truly enough resources to feed several times the current world population. But as long as a minority of the world's population demands large quantities of meat, there is going to be a life and death struggle for food somewhere in the world.

The Social Cause Diet extends an invitation to each of us to incorporate service into our lives as a way of healthier living. I would like to propose that we can also eat in ways that are life-giving. Gifted with free will, we have choices. I can write this article, or not. You can read it, or not. We can eat two all-beef patties with special sauce, lettuce, cheese, pickles, and onions on a sesame seed bun—or not. We can plunder the earth's natural resources in order to feed our cravings, or we can choose to adopt environmentally sustainable practices. The worthiest choices consider not only how those choices impact our own self, but also how they impact others.

I encourage individuals to make a difference by going meatless for at least one day out of the week or one week out of the month. Your body, as well as the planet, will appreciate your decrease in meat consumption since less meat translates into a reduced risk of cancer and heart disease, our nation's leading cause of death. But no one is going to insist that you cut back on meat; it's a voluntary act.

Volunteering has been shown to contribute to better health. Studies show that serving something other and greater than ourselves nourishes us physically, mentally, and spiritually. Interestingly, the healthiest subpopulation group is pregnant women. Through compassion for their unborn children, women take better care of themselves during pregnancy than at any other time in their lives, caring more about the life growing within them than for themselves.

It is this same willingness to serve something greater than ourselves that can drive our behaviors toward increased individual, communal, and global health.

When I was pregnant with my first child, I meditated upon this fact and had an image of being pregnant with the earth, connected by a cosmological umbilical cord, which both nourishes and removes waste. Amazingly, the human body is, indeed, a microcosm of the earth, composed of the same elements in the same proportion: three quarters water and one quarter solid, organic and inorganic.

The image in my mind then extended such that every one of us was pregnant with the earth. Buddhist Monk Thich Nhat Hahn says, "Even if you do not have a baby in your womb, the seed is already there. Even if you are not married, even if you are a man, you should be aware that a baby is already there, the seeds of future generations are already there."

Mentally placing the earth within our body helps remind us of our intimate connection with the natural world and our dependence upon it for survival. We could also imagine ourselves in the womb and consider the fact that humans survive only within the larger complex of ecosystems. We cannot be healthy ourselves without a healthy earth. To that end, food provides us with a lifetime of opportunities to show compassion with our dietary choices.

How will you volunteer to eat today?

Lisa Ota is founder of SacredBite where she aspires to nourish one's relationship with food for the benefit of individual, communal and environmental well-being. Visit www.sacredbite.com and sign up for her seasonal newsletters.

Loving The Main

BY BILL HAYES

I could list lots of reasons for loving the Main branch of the San Francisco Public Library, such as the amazing new self-service machines for returning and checking out books, the newly renovated atrium, or the splendid reserve system. But the main thing I've come to love about The Main is simply that it accommodates everyone— and I do mean everyone. Of course, not everyone agrees with me.

"Oh, I never go there anymore," said a woman I met at a party the other night. "All the homeless people! It's so awful, isn't it!"

Well, no, I don't think so, I thought to myself.

True, there are lots of homeless and mentally ill people who find refuge at The Main, especially on rainy or cold days. But if you go, as I do at least once a week, you will see that most often these folks are quietly reading and using the library, not bothering anyone. Sure, they may be whiling away the day (since they don't necessarily have homes of their own to while in), but I am always moved by how often they are putting their time to good use—browsing, reading, watching DVDs or listening to music with headphones, using the internet, and so on.

While doing research for *The Anatomist,* I used to spend long days in the microfilm reading room up on the fifth floor. Over time, I got to know the tics and quirks of each microfilm projector as well as those of the microfilm-reading regulars, many of whom appeared to be homeless patrons. Sometimes I'd help someone with an especially finicky machine; sometimes, he or she would return the favor. What characters! I'll never forget the guy going through box after box of microfilms of The Times of London from the early 20th century. Who knows why? Maybe he was English, maybe he was pursuing his own private obsession. Whatever the reason, I say God bless him.

And bless the librarians and security guards, too! They have tough jobs some days, having to handle those occasional drug-addled or unwell patrons who cannot be shushed with a polite finger to the lips. For instance, last week I was back on the fifth floor getting some help from a librarian when a disheveled older gent walked up and started talking loudly and incoherently about who-knows-what.

"John! John?! Now, you listen here," the librarian said, addressing the man forcefully (but, respectfully, you'll notice, using his name, as he was clearly a regular). "John, you need to lower your voice and wait your turn, okay?"

"Okay," he whispered.

And after she'd finished helping me, she smiled and said, "Okay John, what can I do for you today, dear?"

Bill Hayes is the author of *The Anatomist: A True Story of Gray's Anatomy, Sleep Demons: An Insomniac's Memoir* and *Five Quarts: A Personal and Natural History of Blood.* As for the Main, it welcomes volunteers. Consider volunteering at your local library.

Accidental Family

My Journey From Reluctant Foster Parent to Adoptive Mom

BY JESSICA BROPHY

When the phone rang I was covered in green paint. The living room needed to be freshened up, and I was in the mood for a change after everything we had been through. Saying goodbye to our two young foster children had been more difficult than my husband, Sean, and I anticipated. We were looking forward to some time to recalibrate as a family with our two-year-old daughter, Hailey.

I carefully picked up the receiver, trying not to smear paint on it. "Hello?" I was surprised to hear the voice of our social worker on the other end of the phone. We had asked her not to call us for at least a month, but she was really in a bind.

"I need somebody to take in these two girls just for the weekend," she pleaded. "The foster parents didn't give me any notice." As she filled me in on the details, I could think of a hundred reasons to say no: The girls were eight and ten—much older than we were equipped for. I was only in my twenties and still learning how to parent toddlers. These girls had severe behavior issues and had been through four foster homes in as many weeks. Besides, I was in the middle of painting.

But she was persuasive. After all, it would only be for one weekend.

Toni and Jessica arrived the next morning with everything they owned in tow. It seemed like a lot of stuff for one weekend, but I cheerfully showed them to their room. Hailey peeked around the corner with great curiosity and ran away squealing each time one of the girls made eye contact with her.

"So where's my new school?" Toni asked after putting her things away. Sean shot me a pointed look. What had I gotten us into this time? "I'll call the social worker on Monday morning," I assured him as soon as the girls were out of earshot. "She'll have something else lined up by then."

She didn't.

The months that followed were some of the most difficult times I had ever experienced. Sean and I prayed fervently for God's leading as we struggled through the tantrums and intense anger the girls began to unleash. Many times we were tempted to give up, but every so often there was a glimmer of hope that things would improve.

One afternoon I noticed that Toni and Jessica were unusually quiet as we drove home from school. When they sat down to start their homework, Jessica fidgeted and tapped her pencil nervously.

"OK, what's going on," I asked. They looked at each other hesitantly.

"Why can't we call you Mom?" Toni blurted out.

I was stunned. The girls spent most of their time contradicting me and complaining about my cooking. But Hailey could hardly remember life before the arrival of her "sissies." Could it be that in spite of the challenges we were actually becoming a family?

That night Sean and I sat on the edge of their beds as we prayed with them. I glanced around at the patched holes where Jessica had kicked the walls during her tantrums. It had been a tumultuous start for all of us, but somehow love happened.

"Goodnight Mom, Goodnight Dad." Toni smiled, and our eyes met before I turned out the light.

"I love you," I whispered.

The social worker was thrilled when Sean and I inquired about adopting the girls. It had become clear that reunification with their biological family was not a viable option. "Oh, by the way," she added, "is there any way you could pick up Lacey tomorrow for the visit?"

A tremendous sense of dread washed over me as I reluctantly agreed. Lacey was bad news. She was the girls' older sister, and she had been assigned to a group home because of her unruly behavior. At fourteen she was well on her way to a life of degeneracy. If Toni and Jessica had obstacles to overcome, Lacey made their problems seem trivial. She was not a good influence on her sisters, and I did everything I could to keep their contact minimal. The once-a-month visits, however, were court-ordered.

"Whassup?" mumbled Lacey as she hopped into the back seat of my car. The hood of her sweatshirt was pulled over her head, and she slumped into her seat, her eyes cast downward. Her clothes smelled like cigarettes, and I cracked the window in spite of the cold weather.

"Hi Lacey." I eyed her cautiously in the rearview mirror. "How was your Christmas?"

"It was cool," she replied blandly. She went on to tell me that all of the other kids had gone home on visits, and she spent the morning watching MTV alone. She received one present from the county, which she opened alone in her room, and then ate a turkey TV dinner. Alone.

I nodded sadly, unsure of what to say. She shrugged it off as if it was no big deal, but I could see the pain in her eyes. Somebody needed to do something about her.

A couple of days later I opened my Bible and Psalm 68:4-5 seemed to leap off the page at me: "A father to the fatherless, a defender of widows is God in his holy dwelling. God sets the lonely in families…" The words were like an arrow through my heart.

I thought of Lacey, and how she spent Christmas morning. Here I was, building my happy family from the remnants of her shattered life while she remained desperately alone. How could I have been so selfish? I hadn't even sent her a card. God was a father to the fatherless and a defender of widows, but he didn't just comfort them with flowery words of love. He sent his people. He set them in families. Families like mine.

I dropped to the floor and cried my heart out. I was so sorry that I hadn't been there for her. I was so sorry that I hadn't encouraged her sisters to call. So sorry that I had failed to see her as the wounded child that she was. I vowed that things would be different from here on out. I would be different—and I would never be the same.

When I finally dried my eyes I stood up with a new sense of purpose. It would complicate our lives, but I was certain that God was leading me to bring Lacey into our home. I couldn't wait to share my new insight with Sean.

"What?" Sean asked incredulously. "You have got to be kidding! There is no way that kid is coming to live here! No way! We have Hailey and Toni and Jessica to worry about." He was becoming pretty irritated as he listed all of the reasons why a rational person would not even suggest such a thing.

I felt defeated. I went for a walk to clear my head and pray. If Lacey were meant to be with us, Sean would have to have a change of heart. That night I asked him if he would be open to having Lacey spend the weekend with us. "That might be OK," he answered, "as long as it's just for the weekend."

One weekend led to several more visits, and soon Sean began to feel as passionately as I did that Lacey should come to stay. The conditions at the group home were horrible, and we believed that many of her problems were a result of her environment. What she needed was to be part of a real family. Her social worker vehemently disagreed.

"I wish I could tell you a success story about somebody like Lacey," she told us, "but there's not one."

The situation escalated, and we found ourselves embroiled in an emotionally draining battle for Lacey's future. In fact, the future of our whole family was at stake. The adoption worker for Toni and

Jessica put our case on hold, informing us that our stance with Lacey could jeopardize their adoptions as well. I was devastated. As we prepared to go to court to oppose the county's recommendations, I held fast to Psalm 68:5. I prayed silently while we awaited the judge's decision. God, let your will be done.

Lacey's adoption was finalized on June 24, 2005, one year after the adoptions of Toni and Jessica. She was sixteen years old and barely resembled the bitter, wounded child she once was. The courtroom was packed with those who had encouraged us during our difficult yet rewarding journey.

I was very proud of Lacey and her resiliency despite the difficulties she had faced in her young life. But perhaps the biggest change had occurred in my own heart.

Jessica Brophy is a freelance writer, singer/songwriter and taxi-mom to an ever-changing number of children. She currently leads worship at God's House church in Vallejo, CA.

How to be a Kick-Butt Volunteer

BY SHYLA BATLIWALLA

In lieu of a story, I would like to contribute the results of my extensive and remarkable research. A volunteer, by definition, serves and improves our community. But a little birdie once told me there are some volunteers who prefer to laze around and play Candy Land instead of getting any real work done. I assume these people believe that since they are volunteering, they are automatically helping and consequently forget to put genuine sweat into their work.

Is it possible to have your peacock feathers a bit too fully displayed and misdirect your admirable intentions? I posed the following questions to a bunch of my cronies who have years of experience in the nonprofit sector: What makes a first-rate volunteer? What makes a helplessly high-maintenance volunteer? How can a person become a super-hero volunteer?

Listen to the following advice of my friends. I'll be bold enough to guarantee that my grass-roots amigos can steer you down the most direct boulevard to becoming a kick-butt volunteer.

Jennifer Beahrs, a TEACH FOR AMERICA alumnus who spent a year teaching children living in poverty in India, gives three pointers:

■ Good volunteers take their work as seriously as they would if they were getting paid. Bad volunteers think they are a big help no matter what they do because they're not getting paid. This results in disappointed colleagues who rely on volunteers to be responsible.

- Good volunteers are doing it because they believe in the mission. Bad volunteers are doing it because it looks good on their resumé (or because they have the hots for another volunteer).

- Good volunteers "know when to hold 'em and know when to fold 'em" (according to Kenny Rogers, *The Gambler*). They know when to "step up" to responsibility as needed and when it's time to "step down" a bit to let someone else make a decision.

William Most, Harvard graduate, environmental activist and pro pedal boat racer offers his three:

- Be proactive! It's not easy for organizations to figure out how best to use volunteers, so actively figure out ways to contribute and be useful.

- Help raise money! Throw fundraisers. Consider making a deal with a local bar who agrees to donate a dollar from every drink on a certain day, and then invite all your friends to join you for a happy hour. What's better then getting boozed up while raising cash for a good cause?

- Let them know if you are coming or not! It's okay if you have to flake—but be sure the organizer knows ahead of time.

Faye Johnson, a native of South Africa who interned with HUMAN RIGHTS WATCH and currently works on foreign affairs issues for the U.S. government, makes this strong point:

- I never hire anyone who says, "I'll come, but I am ONLY doing *this* or *that*." These people will take more time then they are worth to train because they refuse to jump in where they are needed and don't take initiative. I will ask a potential volunteer how adamant they are about their stipulation—they might just be nervous or underconfident. Nervousness can be remedied by giving assurances. But if the person still seems adamant about doing only one task, and it's a multi-task project, I will look for someone else.

Tara Ebrahimi, who volunteers her summers to work with Native American tribes and makes a mean root beer float for the elderly has this to say:

- The critical thing to remember is that YOU are there to help THEM. Don't be fussy about what you are assigned to do; sometimes it might seem like you're doing something trivial or inane, like stuffing envelopes, but every little thing helps and there are a million little tasks necessary to run an organization.

- Be aware of the "Mother Teresa" syndrome: a longing to help everyone. Overextending yourself in volunteering can leave a yucky taste in your mouth. In my humble estimation, helping one person is a whole lot better than helping a lot of people just a little bit. Plus, you have the power to create a chain of volunteerism.

Lastly, my dear friend *Adam Fink,* a true humanitarian who recently returned from two years in Africa where he worked with the organization INVISIBLE CHILDREN, took my research very seriously. He came up with the following:

ADAM FINK'S TEN COMMANDMENTS FOR VOLUNTEERS

1. **Be purposeful.** Know what skills you have to contribute before you arrive on the scene.

2. **Be flexible.** This includes being prepared to do administrative grunt work. (Sorry, not all aid work involves washing babies and hugging orphaned children.)

3. **Be reflective.** Constantly question your motives. Ask yourself why you are helping, think of your motivation, and keep that at the forefront of your mind.

4. **Be receptive.** Learn as much as you can. That said, be wary of engaging for too long with veterans who have become hardened and cynical from their work. Instead, find long-termers with hope still gleaming in their eyes. Then, latch on with open ears.

5. **Be positive.** Take pride in your idealism—you need it to ward off cynicism's approach to your difficult environment.

6. **Be realistic.** Your idealism can be balanced only by the knowledge that you are not here to save the world, but to play one specific role and that you may never witness the effects of your efforts.

7. **Be independent.** Much of your work will depend on your personal initiative. Be a team player, but do not rely on others to guide you every step of the way.

8. **Be empathetic.** Your ability to succeed will depend upon your connection to and understanding of the people you work with.

9. **Be humble.** Don't speak much. Listen. Avoid grandiose conclusions about a problem, community, or philosophy that you were recently introduced to. Act. Think. Feel. But don't come to too many conclusions—they will only halt your experiential learning process.

10. **Have a ball.** Just be sure you've earned it.

In conclusion, it is possible for a person to show up in his or her best volunteering outfit with polished teeth shining and end up being more of a pain in the tushie. Before you start bragging about your work with near-sighted orphans, take a moment to reflect upon your involvement. It's best to make sure that your exertions match your intentions before you go forth and save the world!

A version of this article first appeared on DivineCaroline.com, a place where people can publish stories about anything that matters to them. Read more and share your own stories at www.divinecaroline.com. Be sure to check out the area called Neighborhood & World.

Inside Addition

BY JES STEINBERG

There are only four of us this year. Four. That number keeps running through my head. It is less than a handful, and I can't fathom the thought process of those who have bailed out. Are we really to a point in our lives where we are so busy we can no longer make time for the rest of the world? I am struck with a feeling that no one cares but me. With low expectations by my side, we begin the trek south of the border. The only thing that excites me is that my fifteen-year-old brother is on this trip. My hope is that he will have a life-altering experience in these next few days; that he will come back changed, the way that I did so many years ago.

Out of my seven mission trips, three have been to Rancho De Sus Ninos, a place that began as an orphanage and grew to become a center for many needful services to families in the Tijuana area. I love returning and seeing how the kids have grown and which ones are still there. I feel more connected with Rancho than with other places I've served where I built houses in the middle of nowhere for families I would never see again. Although the futures of those families who now have roofs over their heads changed forever, I never got to see it. I'm reminded that it is not about me, and I begin to examine my motives and why I even come on these trips in the first place...

A seasoned vet, I am not shocked when we get a flat tire on Highway 5. I'm not shocked when this sets us back a few hours, when we get lost, or when we show up so late that we can't find anyone on the property to open the gates and let us in. We search around the dorm area for unlocked doors and vacant rooms and find three beds for which we are thankful. Mike, our fearless leader, sleeps in the van by the side of the road. I wonder if this is the first time this has happened. He's made several trips down here, and his willingness to serve selflessly always astounds me.

We wake up to the bright sun shining through the curtainless windows. We are tired, hungry and under-caffeinated. After concocting a Mexican Mocha or two, we sit down to eat and are welcomed by another group that is there from the States. I am unaware of it at the time, but these six men will be our saving grace. We are there because of them; they are there because of us.

We go to a church service at the orphanage on Saturday night, wearing jeans and t-shirts and not thinking anything of it. We sit in the back row of the meeting area where the service is being held. Ten minutes later, at least seven rows of chairs have been added behind us, and every seat in the house is taken. Most people have driven a long way to get here, and each of them is making me feel more underdressed than I have ever felt in my life—not because their clothes are better than mine, but because it is obvious that they are all wearing their best. Although they have no translator and I can only decipher every ninth word they are singing and saying, the presence of God is real and alive in this place. I am overwhelmed with the realization that the God we serve is very present and very international.

Work begins early the next morning. Our group is usually assigned our own project, but because there are so few of us, we latch on to the guys from the States who are working on the hospice building. Initially, this disappoints me; I would much rather be playing with the kids, painting one of their houses or doing something closer to the orphanage. Hanging up sheet rock in the building on top of the hill doesn't sound like a dream job to me, but I am there to serve, so I will do it. We find out that the six men are from Washington, and they make quarterly trips to Rancho. They are all experts in construction or electrical work, even the ones who are too humble to admit it.

Our instructions are to remove all of the sheet rock that was recently hung, install insulation and then re-sheetrock each room. If there is anything that has made less sense to me in my entire life, I cannot think of it after hearing these instructions. My assumption is that the insulation was originally overlooked. I inquire and find out that I am wrong. Initially, they did not have enough money to get the insulation, but they had the sheet rock and workers, so they did what they could. When the head honcho heard about this later, he informed them that insulation is a requirement. My guess is that the insulation is needed to regulate temperature. Later, I find out it has much more to do with sound.

We labor all day, breaking only for lunch, water and an occasional joke or two. The Washington men take my brother under their wing, and I can already see him having fun and growing up while engaged in hard work with good company. The men show us how to remove sheet rock, how to cut and install insulation, and how to re-sheetrock. We find out that they were the ones who hung the sheet rock the last time they were there. I can't imagine doing such a huge job, only to return months later and be asked to undo it.

Day two I realize what we are doing. We are not just hanging up sheet rock and picking up nails. We were providing people with a dignified place to die. This was not going to be a medical facility, full of hopeful nurses and sterile towels and hospital corners; it was going to be a loud, sometimes disgusting, groan-filled place to house people in their last weeks, days, hours. Nonetheless, it was a place. It was somewhere for them to go. It was there, being built and torn down, and rebuilt—and we were needed to make it happen.

Generally, when I go on a mission trip, I take about a zillion photos to show the progress of the work—pictures that tell the story of what we did in this far, far away land. I have scrapbooks and slideshows and folders on my computer full of these proofs. I often look over them, remembering putting shingles on a roof or painting an odd color on the walls of a classroom. There is a feeling of satisfaction in a job well done; completion in seeing the work you have built with your own hands.

This is not the case in this story. If I was to take before and after pictures of walls with sheet rock, and then walls with insulation and sheet rock, there would be absolutely no external difference. The photos would look exactly the same. The only thing that would be different is what is on the inside—that which cannot be seen, but that which we know is there.

To volunteer at Rancho De Sus Ninos, visit www.ranchodesusninos.org. Similar foundations can be found. Consider www.corazondevida.org or www.aguaviva.com. Jes encourages folks to go during school months when there are fewer volunteers.

A Light Change

BY AVERY HAIRSTON

I am a founder of RelightNY. I'm sixteen years old. About a year ago, I teamed up with friends I have had since kindergarten to see what we could do to help the environment. We came up with RelightNY. Our mission is very simple: inspire as many people as possible to replace their incandescent light bulbs with *compact fluorescent light bulbs*—also called CFLs. CFLs are much more energy-efficient. Although they are more expensive up-front, they last ten times longer. And since they use less energy, there's actually a savings from lower electricity bills.

We raise money from just about anyone—from classmates to corporations—because not everyone can afford the initial cost of switching to CFLs. So far, we have raised enough money to purchase and donate 21,000 of these light bulbs to families in low-income housing.

One of the greatest things about my experience with RelightNY is seeing how people respond when they discover they can make a difference. Last summer I returned to the first housing unit where we donated these light bulbs. I met a woman who told me that not only did she buy more light bulbs for the rest of her house, but she also unplugged all of her electronic appliances when they were not in use and shut off her air conditioning for the entire summer. She was pleased and proud to be doing her part to conserve energy.

Most people my age feel powerless when they hear phrases like "global warming" and "climate crises." My friends and I don't even drive yet. We can't go out and buy hybrids or put solar panels on our roofs. But it's simpler than all that. It's about making little changes that add up to a big impact, and helping other people do the same.

For more information on RelightNY or to help the boys reach their goal of donating one million light bulbs before they graduate, go to www.relightNY.com.

Malcolm—In Memoriam

BY LARRY NILSON

I have made it a practice in my life to reach out to people who at first seem a bit different. I am often blessed by such efforts as I discover the deeper interests and gifts of these new friends.

I first met Malcolm at a church Bible study. Sometimes hesitant in speech and a bit hard to understand, he seemed a simple man. He lived in public housing in a neighboring town in Massachusetts and often walked several miles to church even in poor weather. This impressed me. Through our months of sharing in class, I gradually saw him in a new way, hardly simple, but a man of wisdom and faith who was continually growing.

In the years that followed, we developed a deep respect for one another. We shared meals together and often talked on the phone. I sometimes picked him up or gave him a ride home. These were good times when we freely discussed opinions, broad ideas and concerns. Malcolm loved people, nature, music, poetry and travel, probably in that order. Sometimes he would call to recite a recent poem he had written, reluctant to bother me, but eager to share. He composed songs, taught himself to play a few instruments, and carried around a little notebook to record his ideas and insights for his writing.

Without being able to drive, and with seemingly little worldly experience, Malcolm found a way to travel far and wide, always with a definite purpose and well-laid plans. He cared deeply for the marginalized peoples of the world. Once, he went to India with the intent of meeting Mother Teresa. There he visited the Sisters of

Charity and met Mother Teresa's assistants. The smiles, calm and peace he experienced there made a deep impression on him. I think Mother Teresa was a model for Malcolm, for it was his commitment as a volunteer that was most amazing. Almost every weekday he would help in a nursing home, assist at Children's Hospital, or teach recent immigrants. I was so pleased when the United Methodist Women chose him for their special mission award. It was a proud moment for Malcolm and he thanked the women by playing "Count Your Many Blessings" on his harmonica. Everyone was especially moved by his impromptu performance because they knew he was not well.

Malcolm kept his initial struggles with cancer largely hidden. Over the years, we had been open and frank about medical issues but he downplayed this one. He had pain way beyond what was evident, keeping his smile and optimism through great discomfort. Only during the last few months did Malcolm share his pain with me and seem to need my hugs and offerings of support.

Then came the day when I found Malcolm lying on his sweaty bed in his dark bedroom. He was moaning. It was a scene of suffering and dying. He accepted my presence and help but was too ill for conversation. He said he hurt but was okay. I knew he was in pain, but maybe he suffered less than others might under the same circumstances. Probably his deep faith and acceptance sustained him.

I thought about how to serve my friend and a picture of the Last Supper came to mind when Jesus washed the feet of his disciples, his friends. Jesus wasn't just teaching by example. It was more than that. He was giving his disciples another eucharist—"This is my body I have given you." What I saw here with Malcolm was a calling to do the same.

The giving of oneself can be physical, such as the service of yard work or the delivery of a meal to someone who is housebound, or it can be psychological and relational, such as listening, teaching or entering into a difficult interaction for the purpose of bringing peace and resolution. While I usually find the latter service to be more difficult, this day, I was to be challenged by the former.

Quietly, I began to clean Malcolm's apartment and straighten up. I washed the dishes and cleaned the stove, sink and refrigerator. The cupboards were nearly bare. What did he eat? Previously, when I had asked Malcolm what he needed at the store, he would say that he was fine. Now I knew I would have to be more persistent in the future.

So far, my efforts to serve my friend had been easy, but cleaning the bathroom was another matter entirely. Soiled clothes and towels, the sink and the toilet presented an extreme challenge. With lots of patient effort, hot water and a paint scraper, I was able to work through thick layers of soap on the porcelain sink. The toilet required rubber gloves and full strength cleaning agents. The heat, odors and lack of ventilation were nearly unbearable. With my sweaty face practically in the toilet bowl, I labored to achieve some degree of cleanliness and order for my friend. Eventually I was back at his side. I think he was too ill to be embarrassed by the conditions I had found and for that I was grateful. It was hard enough to watch him suffer.

This experience of "foot washing" provided an important foundation for the months ahead as I supported Malcolm in different ways. He was moved to a new "home" at a local facility where I visited daily. We talked and sometimes we both dozed. We would constantly shift his pillows and change the tilt of the bed, hoping for some relief. When he was up to it, I would read his poetry to him. Sometimes we prayed together. Malcolm never failed to pray for his nurses, his aides and his hospice "angel." To the end he prayed for strength to remain positive in his suffering.

I will always remember Malcolm as a great gift to me. He enriched my life and my spirit, even as I assisted him in his final journey. Largely because of Malcolm—his friendship, his inspiring life of service and the experience of being with him in his last days—

I've recently accepted the position as a Lay Pastor for those in need in my community. Although I hope I don't have any more bathrooms to clean, I am willing to be a eucharist—a servant—bringing all I am to another and being blessed myself in the process.

SERVE

BY COLLEEN D.C. MARQUEZ

The Lord has told you, human, what is good;

HE HA**S** TOLD YOU

WHAT H**E** WANTS FROM YOU:

TO DO WHAT IS **R**IGHT TO OTHER PEOPLE,

LO**V**E BEING KIND TO OTHERS,

AND LIV**E** HUMBLY, OBEYING YOUR GOD.

Micah 6:8

The Spirit of a Child

BY KAREN HENRICH

As a photographer, I capture images of children through my lens. When you look at the photos I take, you see children through my eyes. You see freckles, bruises, tears and giggles—because these are the things I celebrate in children and capture on film.

But it is through the eyes of children themselves that we see what is truly important. To see the world through the eyes of a child is to see a world filled with wonder, joy, excitement, love, purity, peace, curiosity and even defiance.

I believe that all children are full of such wonder, no matter where they are in terms of physical development—or health.

Eleven years ago, my best friend gave birth to a terminally ill child. I had been planning on capturing the first moments of her baby's life, thinking the photos would be the first of many I would take of my friend's new family member. Instead, I ended up taking the first and *only* pictures of the baby. These photos turned out to be more valuable than any of us had anticipated. They became my friend's primary keepsake of the treasured moments she had with her baby.

After this experience, I began contacting social workers and hospice organizations to volunteer my photography services for others who have children with life-limiting illnesses. The response was immediate and the need was greater than I could manage on my own. I formed a nonprofit organization called Moment by Moment to bring together other professional photographers who would be willing to serve in this way. Now with a cadre of over 100 professional photographers, we have captured precious images of more than 600 children and their families. Together, we have discovered that the spirit of a child does not reside in their illness. Through our lenses, when pointed at these courageous children, we capture a spirit that still radiates hope, determination, and an unbreakable connection with their families. And we capture those wonderful expressions that parents may take for granted or may in the future have a difficult time remembering.

The first question people often ask us is, "Why take portraits for a family during such a hard time, when the child is sick?" But what we've found is that, more than ever, these families want to document and celebrate what they have this day, this moment.

Additionally, it a blessing *to me* to work with these families. After each shoot, I am grateful that on this day, I did not have to comfort my own child in the confines of hospital walls. I am grateful that on this day, I did not have to meet with a team of specialists, who—no matter how much training they have—cannot tell me for certain if my child will be "fine." I am grateful that on this day, I can enjoy a workout or a coffee with a friend, without feeling that I should instead be at my child's bedside. I am grateful to be on the outside, as a photographer, capturing memories of children who make an indelible mark on this world, although here for such a short while.

I go home from each shoot and tell my two boys how much I love them. They typically respond with, "Mom, we love you more." I explain that cannot possibly be true! And again, I am grateful—grateful for this little ritual and the moments we have to share it.

For more information on Moment by Moment, go to www.momentbymoment.org.
Karen Henrich, founder, portrait photographer and mother, recently authored three books:
The Wonder of Girls, *The Wonder of Babies* and *The Wonder of Boys*.

Confessions of a Peace Corps Volunteer

BY NIKKI MAXWELL

After four years of college, studying long hours and reading until my eyes felt like they were on fire, I decided to defy my father's wishes to work for a paycheck. I decided to join the Peace Corps.

People ask me why. Why? Easy! It simply felt right. Don't get me wrong—I wouldn't recommend doing something as life changing as Peace Corps without first doing your research, but I did none. I just knew it was something I had to do for purely selfish reasons. It was something I wanted to do to make myself a better person. It was as simple as that.

The assignment: to work in primary schools as a teacher trainer in the newly established post-apartheid Republic of South Africa. Now, I could tell you that I loved every minute of it. I could tell you it made me want to fight for the rights of children everywhere. I could even tell you that I became fluent in SiSwati, the language spoken in the region in which I worked.

But the truth is, I was scared out of my mind the first few months I was at my Peace Corps site. I kept thinking, did I really just sign up for this? Did someone drop me on my head as a child and make me lose all sensible reasoning? Did they get my resume and application mixed up with another volunteer's application? What in the world am I doing here? What in the heck was I thinking? You know, sensible thoughts.

After my first day at one of the schools, the kids thought a huge joke had been played on them. They were told a person from America was there to assist them with their education. Then they saw me, and said, "How can she be from America? She is black!" I panicked and thought, "The jig is up! They hate me already and I haven't even opened my mouth. YIKES!" But the opposite happened. They were in awe that someone who looked liked them lived in this foreign place called America—the place where, as the kids explained it to me, everyone is rich.

I cannot even begin to tell you how much the children affected me there in South Africa. All odds stacked against them and they still managed to come to school on time every day, walking in torn shoes kilometer after kilometer and wearing smiles on their faces when peanut butter was spread on one piece of bread for their lunch. What did I, a twenty-two year old female from the suburbs who had all her needs granted, have to teach them?

After two months, a group of seventh grade girls began to visit me while I worked in the office. There were seven or eight of them who would show up daily and ask me questions. They asked things any seventh grade girl would ask: Do you have children? Are you married? How many sisters and brothers do you have? What music do you like?

They also asked more surprising things like, "How much would your lobola be?" I'd answer, "50 cows!" Since the standard lobola (dowry) was only five cows, I'd wink at them and add, "Just like you, I'm expensive."

Many of the girls couldn't believe I thought they were worth 50 cows. I told them they were worth more than they thought. They would say, "No Nikki, you are worth a thousand cows, but not me!" That caused me to feel uneasy and unworthy again. I didn't think I was worth even being there, but these amazing girls were putting me on a pedestal. I wished they would place themselves on a pedestal.

So one day I decided to turn the tables and have the girls ask each other questions. One girl in the group would be 'in the spotlight' for an hour during each afternoon visit. To make it somewhat of a writing exercise, I instructed the girls to come prepared with notes about why they liked the girl who was to be spotlighted that day.

I tell you, the first day in implementing this exercise was nerve-wracking. No one wanted to speak. After one full minute of staring at each other (it's amazing how long a minute is in complete silence), I said, "Well, I think Jabu has beautiful eyes." The girls took their cues and said every other part of Jabu's body was beautiful. Jabu was beautiful from her eyebrows down to her toenails. Someone even said her elbow was beautiful. It was an excellent language lesson for me because I learned how to say every body part in SiSwati! But finally, when no other body parts could be given, one brave soul said, "I think Jabu has a beautiful heart." I cry at anything, but I held back the small tear, smiled, and asked, "Why do you think that?" She answered, "Because she is my sister and best friend. I love her."

It took off after that. Could they have been trying to compete with each other to see who could make the Peace Corps volunteer cry? Perhaps. If they were, they were all winners. The teachers told me later that my girls became more confident in their classrooms, asking more questions and sharing more often. Their friendships grew so tight they began to look out for each other both inside and outside of school.

By the end of that year, I did not want to say goodbye to them. It hurt to know I would not see them five days out of the week. I almost felt embarrassed to be so sad over losing the company of seventh graders. I felt like I was saying farewell to my best friends before moving to a new school—if you have ever had this experience, you know how sad it is.

The girls did so much more for me than they will ever realize. They made me feel like a better person. And it was as simple as that.

 This story first appeared on DivineCaroline.com, a place where people can publish stories about anything that matters to them. To research the Peace Corps, visit www.peacecorps.gov.

A Two Hour Walk
With Grandma Bette

BY BETTE SIMONS

Often, it's a boy who wants to get ahead of me as I lead a string of first graders up a hill in our California chaparral forest. I use my firm voice acquired during my younger days as a teacher to stop the renegade from passing me. Then I like to say, "Do you want to be the leader? That's great! Maybe you will be a wonderful leader some day. But first you must learn how to follow."

As a grandma, I move slowly, but that is entirely appropriate when learning from the great outdoors. It proves helpful when teaching young visitors the value of being still for observation. The Children's Nature Institute, located in the Santa Monica Mountains in Southern California, is a nonprofit organization that teaches schoolchildren about the local mountains that are so close to their urban home. If 75% of the children at a school are on the free lunch program, the Institute gives the kids, their teachers, and their parents a free bus ride and field trip to explore the area. We are a collection of nature experts, child care professionals, and young-to-old volunteers, warmly welcoming bus loads of students to the particular park site that has been chosen for them.

Many of these children have never been in the mountains before; they have never before left the inner-city chaos, pollution and concrete. Prior to their trip, our Wonder Mobile visits their school and introduces them to a bevy of items to prepare them for what they might find in nature's playground. From animal skulls to stuffed birds to tarantulas, they are intrigued and ready to see more.

Once an eager child ask me if he would see a shark in the stream; later, if we would see Big Foot on the trail. But the children are thrilled enough when we spot a red tailed hawk, darkling beetles or a packrat's nest. They carefully imitate me as I show them how to kiss their hands to talk to the birds and rub a leaf of sage to release its smell.

One day, I suppose I will have to turn in my old hiking boots and stop volunteering. But I know that many of the children I've walked in front of will someday be leaders themselves, teaching others about the wonders of nature and how to care for it.

♡ Dear Grandma Bette,
Thank you for takeing us for a walk. I no the plant closed it leaves to keep the water inside. you are so smart. I did't no that you guys are so cool. I hope I can see you agine in nature.

Your friend, ♡
Amanda

For more about The Children's Nature Institute, go to www.childrensnatureinstitute.org. For other outdoor volunteer opportunities, go to www.volunteermatch.org and do a search (using your zipcode) with the keyword "outdoor" or "recreation."

Pack Pencils

BY PATRICIA COSTELLO

Last March I visited Guatemala for their "Semana Santa" (Holy Week). I had the opportunity to accompany a tour group as they visited a Mayan family in the town of Santiago de Atitlan in the highlands of the country. Hugo, our tour guide, banged on a piece of corrugated metal that served as a side wall to the family's humble home. In this part of town, everything is loosely constructed out of corrugated metal.

A small boy, about age six, pulled open a separated piece of metal that was used as a door and greeted us with a smile that measured almost the diameter of his head. He welcomed us in, one by one, taking us by the hand and escorting us into a tiny courtyard with a dirt floor. There, his parents and siblings worked on foot looms creating colorful weavings. They were colorful themselves, especially the women who proudly wore their traditional dress of long wrap-around skirts and intricately woven needlepoint tops.

Before I left for Guatemala, the tour company had sent me a brochure outlining precautions and basic information about the country. One paragraph mentioned that children were very grateful to receive paper and pencils. I wasn't clear on this point, but one woman in our group was. She had traveled extensively in Latin America and always brought along pens, pencils and tiny spiral notepads that the children could use in school.

I was so glad to have been informed because even though we were at the home in large part to purchase a weaving or two, it would have been awkward to arrive empty-handed. The children were so happy to receive these gifts. Tools for an education are luxury items for those who struggle to eke out a living.

Throughout my trip I met doctors, nurses, dentists and even a veterinarian who were all traveling in Guatemala for the sole purpose of tending to the needs of the impoverished people of this country. It was comforting to know that so many professionals cared enough to give their time for such a worthy cause. I was just as moved to realize that such a simple thing as a piece of paper or a pencil could make a difference in someone's life as well. Maybe I didn't have a professional skill to offer, but I could pass out pencils!

Patricia Costello is a teacher and writer. She is presently finishing a work of crime fiction set in Panama. In addition to pencils, other items you can pack to give away when traveling to other countries are small puzzles, hair accessories, toothbrushes, flashlights, and jewelry. Speaking of jewelry, some cultures are very generous, even if poor, so be careful how you complement a person: If you tell a woman that you admire her necklace, for example, she may take it off and give it to you!

"It is good to feel and name and express feelings."
Cassandra, student

Writing Through the Darkness

BY ELIZABETH MAYNARD SCHAEFER

A dozen people chat as they pull chairs around the conference table, organize purses and backpacks, and pull out pens and notebooks. Tallest is Harry, an engineer who's been unable to work for several years; next to him is Cassandra, a beautiful blond who dropped out of college and desperately dreams of returning to finish her degree; then William, a chemist; and Marion who is hoping to return to teaching soon. Each of these people has an amazing history of a life damaged by chronic depression or bipolar disorder (manic depression). Each has been struck down and each is fighting to get back up, and in this creative writing group I lead, we all lend each other a hand to hold and offer ears to listen.

I've done volunteer work before. I helped a Chinese scholar with his English in college. I taught a newly-immigrated Afghani family basic phrases and sentences to use when buying items at the store. I trained as a reproductive health counselor and volunteered at a women's clinic, discussing pregnancy options and HIV test results. I fed injured baby birds with an eyedropper at a local nature center. Each of these unpaid activities was fascinating and, I believe, made a difference. But with the writing group I created for people with mood disorders, I feel different; this time it feels much more personal.

The importance of writing took hold of me on one of my visits to the hospital with severe depression due to my bipolar disorder. Once again I'd become so despondent that I agreed to stay in this locked ward because I concurred with my doctors and my husband that I probably was a danger to myself. I was in my mid-thirties and had been unable to work for several years due to my debilitating moods, concentration problems and exhaustion. In addition to pills from a whole row of bottles each day, I was receiving shock treatments every few months. Thankfully they helped bring my mood and thinking back to a place near normal, but with each treatment my memory was being eaten away. Now I waited for another treatment, miserable and angry at myself because my life had come to a screeching halt despite my hopes for the long career in science journalism that I had begun. I pulled a notebook from my bedside table. Maybe trying to write down something of my emotions would help as it had on a couple of occasions in my life—but I was unable to think in sentences. I wrote a list of words about my current state instead, and set the book aside. Then it dawned on me that those words had helped some—those quick moments of scribbling changed everything for me.

Back at home several days later, with a less tragic but still sad and confused disposition, I sat on the sofa and wrote some more. I described all the feelings I had about this illness, all the stories I could recall about how it had happened and ideas about what might help or harm me now. And I felt a little calmer, a little more capable. So I wrote more and more, each day journaling about my current state and my earlier life events, good and bad. Soon I began experimenting with other forms, creating poems and stories. I began taking classes and workshops on writing, and reading every writing book I could find. And it helped me; I wasn't over my illness by any means, but I felt less inept, as though perhaps there were something of value left in me after these painful years. Then I came upon a newspaper article one morning about how researchers had found that certain simple writing exercises, done for as little as 20 minutes a day for four days, helped people feel happier and healthier in measurable ways. Amazing! Actual proof of what I had been experiencing. I quickly became an unofficial student of the new field of "writing and healing" and read all I could find on that, too.

Writing every day was more than cathartic for me—it strengthened me. So one summer afternoon I felt bold enough to propose to a clinic researcher an idea I'd had percolating for a long time: I offered to begin a free creative writing group for people with mood disorders, to be held at the Stanford University psychiatry clinic that I already visited every week for my doctor appointments. I wanted to share what I'd experienced with others like me. I wanted to watch them heal, to see them find self-expression amid an illness that stifled it, and to observe as they discovered their voice and even found joy through this creative outlet. Above all, I wanted to take these hellish years and make something of value from them.

In 1998 I began a weekly writing group with a handful of members who had responded to fliers I posted. I quickly learned that I needed to lead, not lecture, for the bulk of what we learned we gained through the writing experience and through sharing with others. I could apply the latest research results as I designed exercises for us to do together, but for the most part, these writers didn't want to listen, they wanted to *do*. The emotional support of the group was phenomenal—people read their work aloud and received validation from their peers by being listened to, even if no comments were made. We all realized what thoughtful, kind, and interesting people we were surrounded by as we sat in a circle in the conference room each week. We were inspired by how each person was striving each day to get just a little healthier and a little closer to the life he or she envisioned without a disabling illness.

We wrote on, season after season. We shared feelings of doom, experiences with doctors and loved ones, childhood hurts, and tips on coping. Sometimes I gave writing assignments on an aspect of our health. (How did you feel when you were first diagnosed with a mental disorder? What do you do when you're depressed? What do you need in order to recover?) Other times, I dreamed up writing assignments that had no obvious connection to our mental conditions. (Describe your first car. Who was your childhood hero? Tell the story of a time you laughed.) Either way, we all learned not to be too surprised when our words on any topic linked back to our mental health. Writing breeds honesty and what needs to be said usually comes up in one way or another.

Today, ten years later, we still meet every Tuesday, now usually about 15 of us, coming from all over the San Francisco Bay Area. Some group members come for a few months as they process some issue or work toward returning to school or a job. Other members have come regularly for years. I admire them all, and I learn from each one of them—their stories, their poise as they read them, and their grace as they reach out to support their peers. Although I have been blessed with much better health these last three years than in the dozen before, I am never given a chance to take that for granted as I hear stories of pain each week. I'm honored to continue this volunteer work, ever learning from my students.

I also continued to write on my own and crafted a memoir of my years of illness: how I'd gone from moderate depressions in graduate school, studying for my Ph.D. in biology, to severe depression, later mixed with occasional mania, voices and hallucinations after graduating; my years of cycling into dangerous despair only to be yanked back by my shock treatments; my pleasure in leading this group; and my dreams for a future where I reach out to more and more people coping with mental illnesses. Much to my delight, my book, *Writing through the Darkness: Easing Your Depression with Paper and Pen* (Celestial Arts, 2008), was recently published. Now I am researching and writing on my next book project as I continue to lead the group and give workshops in other venues. This one very personal volunteer project has given me impetus to keep writing, constant inspiration from wonderful people, a chance to keep learning, and now a career as well.

 For more about *Writing Through the Darkness* and Elizabeth Maynard Schaefer, visit www.WritingThroughTheDarkness.com.

No Staying Quiet

BY SANDRA KAY

Last year I went solo to the Tri Valley Haven's Annual Candlelight Walk in Livermore, but having seen other mother/daughter teams and whole families participating in this candlelight march, I decided this year to invite my ten-year-old daughter.

The whole evening turned into a very special mother/daughter time including dinner, t-shirt-making and the walk which started at 7 p.m. While dining at Strizzi's in downtown Livermore, I decided to converse with my daughter about life in general, but mostly about the meaning and significance of the Tri Valley Haven's Candlelight March.

"Do you know what sexual assault means?" I asked to kick start this awkward conversation. Precious how she moved her head up and down as if to say yes, but out of her mouth came the very honest "No." I wanted to be careful—careful not to overwhelm, but careful also not to under-inform.

"Well, you know how there are some criminals who break into cars and there some criminals who break into houses?" I watched her nodding and kept a close look at her facial expressions and eyes.

"Well, sexual assault is kinda like when someone breaks into your body." I reminded her of the good touch, bad touch lessons at home and school; how our bodies are our very own and just like any of our other private property, but even more so, no one should be breakin' in.

Based on her age, facial expressions, eyes, and my own mommy knowledge and insights, that pretty much concluded the definition portion of our conversation. So I moved on to the next subject.

"Okay…now check this out…when I was a child, and this is even true this very day, if someone broke into your car, you could–and would–tell everyone you ran into. You'd tell your family, friends and neighbors. When you told them, they would look at you with compassion and concern and say, 'Are you okay? That's awful! Have you called the police?' Then everyone would know, and everyone would be extra careful about locking up their cars and keeping an eye out for strangers in the area."

I could see that she agreed. She understood so far.

"Same is true," I continued, "if some criminal broke into your house. You could–and would–tell everyone all about it and everyone would look at you, and listen and show compassion and concern. Then they would become extra careful about locking up their houses and keeping a better lookout for strangers." I could see she clearly understood and agreed, but to make my point, I added one more.

"And same is true if you owned a business, let's say, and someone broke into your store. You'd tell everyone, freely. You'd walk up and down the street and tell just about anyone who would listen, 'My store was broken into last night!' and everyone would feel compassion and concern… " By this time she could finish my sentences.

"BUT!" I said, "Here's the strange thing: when I was child, and this is even partly true to this very day, if some criminal broke into your body—

all the rules changed.

If someone broke into your body, you didn't tell a soul. You weren't allowed to because if you did, you'd be shamed and people would stop being friends with you. They would distance themselves from you, and no one would play with you or come to your house anymore. Do you know what the words stigma or taboo mean?"

Precious again, how her head nodded yes, but her honest eyes and mouth answered, "No." And so I did my awkward best to explain those terms; how people all agree that some things are not to be talked about in public and how you will pay a very high price if you do.

"What a cool deal for the criminal, for the predator," I explained, because not only could he commit the crime, but he could walk around all day without worrying about getting caught because no one would talk about the crime and no one would tell. What have I always told you criminals and predators love?" I asked.

"Silence," she answered.

"That's right!!" I went on, "So when sexual assault was taboo, and victims were stigmatized, that's exactly what the predators wanted! They could commit their crimes and add new victims because no one was watching out for them or calling the police! What a great deal for criminals who break into bodies instead of cars, houses or buildings and what a raw deal for the victims!"

I could see the information registering; her eyes allowing me to continue. "Til one day some very brave and courageous victims said, 'FORGET THAT PROGRAM! I don't care what you think of me or who this makes uncomfortable—this is WRONG, WRONG, WRONG and I'm TELLING!' I'm sure those pioneers—those first few victims who spoke out—paid a high price. But now, year after year, more and more people are becoming brave enough to speak out. Do you wanna know who are some brave victims of sexual assault? Oprah Winfrey! Oprah Winfrey told her entire national TV audience! And Maya Angelou! She told the whole world too! And I'm a survivor of sexual assault and your Auntie Keeshie too. But it's not easy...years and years of silence...and now it's going to take years and years of speaking out. That's what this candlelight march tonight is all about. Most of these people are probably survivors, and they want to help remind others that they can speak out too. Brave people; all of them."

I'm sure I said more...too much...not enough. I'm sure I didn't get it exactly right, but I did my best. She was a great listener.

Afterwards, we still had an hour left to talk about other stuff: homework, softball, friends, crushes, middle school, favorite TV shows, music, birthday parties and summer break plans.

There's something I didn't tell my daughter, but will mention here: As a child, when I told someone a criminal broke into my body, their face contorted as if cockroaches were crawling out of my mouth. As I spoke, they walked backwards, away from me, very abruptly. That kept me pretty quiet for a long, long time.

But even though I offered my daughter an edited, lightweight version of sexual assault, I knew she got it when she—on her own—came up with her t-shirt design. She made a big "SHH!" with a red circle around it and red line through it. NO STAYING QUIET is what it meant. Below that, she wrote the word PEACE.

It took all the strength I had and some help from God not to cry when I saw her wear it.

Many of the other candlelight walkers drew very specific messages on their t-shirts as well. I chose to write, "Heal. Help. Hope." I think this is what we need to do as a society. We need to heal victims and the people who love and care about them. We need to learn about and understand the predators and heal them too. As we heal, we then need to help. Survivors helping victims. And through it all, we need hope: hope that we can make a difference; hope that speaking out will reduce the number of victims; hope that we can learn to live with each other on this planet in a respectful and non-violent way.

The original, unedited version of this story can be found on Sandra's blog, shesayswithasmile.blogspot.com, April 27th, 2008. Information on Tri-Valley Haven can be found at www.trivalleyhaven.org.

The Threshold Choir

BY KATE MUNGER

The inspiration for the Threshold Choir came one day in 1990 while I was caring for my friend Larry, who was comatose yet restless, dying of HIV/AIDS. All morning, I washed dishes, weeded his garden, and organized his quilt fabrics. All afternoon, I sat by his bedside and sang the same song over and over again for hours. As I sang, we both became calmer. At the end of the afternoon, I was sure I had given him a gift—a gift that had come from the deepest and most essential part of myself. As I reflected on the experience, I wondered if other singers might want to give and receive that same kind of gift. After reaching out to friends and other singers, I discovered that there were, indeed, many who were interested in tending to the dying this way, and so began the Threshold Choir.

Today, as we approach our eighth anniversary, there are fifty-two Threshold Choirs across the country performing this healing service. These choirs honor the ancient tradition of singing at the bedsides of people who are struggling, some with living, some with dying. We sing for a diverse group of people: those who are feeble or in a coma, those with end-stage disease, newborns just opening their eyes to the world, and women who are incarcerated.

In December 2007, our Threshold Choir, headquartered in Inverness, California, was asked by an attending nurse if we could hurry over to a nearby home and sing for a family whose baby, named Violet, had just died at the age of two months.

"Yes, of course," I said, and immediately called Pamela, who had sung with the choir five years ago and herself had lost an infant son. Then I called Laura, a lawyer and psychotherapist in San Francisco, who always seems to have the precious few minutes to share for the sake of our singing. When we arrived at the home, the mother, father, and uncle greeted us. The dad was Middle Eastern and the mom and her brother were from Germany. Baby Violet's tiny body was in the bassinet in the center of the living room, wrapped tightly in a blanket surrounded by rose petals and soft toys. We sat close to Baby Violet and started with the St. Francis Prayer—softly, so softly.

"May I be an instrument of Peace...."

For more than thirty minutes, we sang the simplest songs at our softest tone. The family sat together on the couch, each one weeping and holding the others. The father's huge tears tumbled down his cheeks. It was a tremendous honor to give this family a way to express their grief and to honor their baby and her short life.

As we finished, Mom asked if we knew Dona Nobis Pacem. She and her brother sang one part together, beautifully, and we sang the rest. I was so glad we were able to sing together. It was physically and emotionally satisfying to give them something that penetrated to the core of their grief. Three singers, a tiny baby's body, and three grieving family members—intimate, deep, and right in the middle of daily life.

The human voice, our original musical instrument, is a true and gracious vehicle for compassion and comfort. When invited, we visit bedsides a few times a week in small groups and we invite families and caregivers to join us in song or to participate by listening. Our repertoire is chosen to respond to individual musical tastes and might include rounds, chants, lullabies, hymns, spirituals, and classical choral music. Our singing is our gift. Our choir's mission: to provide a container for the grief and give room for the sacred.

 Find out more about the Threshold Choir at www.thresholdchoir.org. The original, unedited version of this story first appeared in *San Francisco Medicine*, the official publication of the San Francisco Medical Society. To learn more, please visit www.sfms.org.

Forgiven

BY KELLIE PAULEY

I walked through the doors of the Alpha Pregnancy Resource Center in the spring of 2003. Little did I know how my good intentions to help others would ultimately have a profound impact on me.

Allow me to back up a bit. I had heard of this nonprofit ministry in the mid 1990s. I was not ready at that time to volunteer. I had all kinds of reasons: small children, part time job, and I was already a volunteer at my children's school. But in reflecting back, it simply was not the right time for me then. I needed to go through some life experiences to become better equipped.

To best understand my story, here is a bit of my history. When I was 16 years old I was in love with my much older boyfriend. I was certain we would get married. We had sex and I got pregnant. He would have married me, but I was hesitant to begin a marriage this way. I convinced him that I must have an abortion. After the procedure, I was never quite the same, nor was he. We broke up shortly thereafter.

Several months after my abortion, I met the man who would later become my husband. I was three months shy of my 18th birthday. After seven years of marriage, at 26, I became a new mother. What should have been a joyous time in my life was overshadowed by fear and sadness. The spring of the following year I made the best decision of my life—I accepted Christ. At this time, I confessed my past sins and felt forgiven—all except for one dark area.

Fast forward to the year 2003. My sons were teens and I was ready to become a volunteer at the pregnancy center. I began as a once-a-week clerk. I assisted the office manager with mailings and did whatever else I could. In order to counsel clients, I signed up for the required four week training course. Once this portion of the training was done, I began an eight week session to confront an issue that I had tried to hide for 20 plus years. I was assigned to a woman who counseled me with love and without judgment. Upon completion, I knew without a doubt I was forgiven and I was free of the guilt and shame I had felt my whole life for having aborted my child.

Part of the fear that had plagued me was "what would my two sons think if they knew my secret?" Would they view me as the hypocrite of all hypocrites? Emboldened by the counseling I received, I shared my history with them individually. Each one told me in his own words "It's ok Mom. That's who you were, not who you are now. I do not love you any less." I am a blessed woman indeed. No more secrets.

Finally I was fully ready to help women facing the same crisis I faced so many years ago. Now in my fourth year of service, I have assisted countless teenagers who come to the center. I educate each one with the truth of fetal development, and with those who chose to parent, I share resources and offer classes on parenting.

Each client must decide for herself what she is going to choose. Some of my former clients have chosen life and now have a sweet son or daughter. Some have chosen an adoption plan for their baby. Others chose to abort. This last choice is one that pains me personally because I know the trauma it causes for years. My new role at the center is to counsel women who are dealing with Post Abortion Syndrome. It is a privilege to see the transformation that happens in a woman's life when she is ministered to in truth and love. I know how it feels—my counselor walked with me through this very process and I am forever grateful and I am forever changed.

 Alpha Pregnancy Resource Centers are located across the country and offer free services to women with unplanned pregnancies. The pomegranate, used as this story's illustration, is an ancient Christian symbol of new life as it bursts open from the abundance of its seeds.

Vision

BY DR. MAITHRI GOONETILLEKE

It was a hot day. Sweat beaded off my skin onto the stethoscope that hung round my neck like the jet black arm of an old friend.

We had been driving for hours over rocky, red clay roads, lined by maize fields and sunflowers.

Giving food. Giving medicine. Giving what love we could.

Late in the afternoon we came to yet another little hut. I looked at the nurses expectantly, with eyes that said… What story will you tell me now? What story of struggle, of hardship, of human beings caught in the fray of life?

In a beautiful soft, Si Swati accent, one exclaimed, "We have heard there is an old man here with untreated TB. He is refusing to come to hospital."

We jumped out of the van and were greeted by a young Swazi man. He told us to follow him.

As the group was walking towards the house, I stopped short.

Huddled in a corner I saw an old woman.

"Who is she?" I asked

"Our Gogo (grandmother)," came the reply from the doorway.

"Why is she sitting like that?"

"Don't worry about her, Sir. She is old now and blind. And that is where she always sits."

"Can she walk?" I persisted.

"Not really. Only a few steps. We bring her food. We take her in to sleep at night."

I knelt down beside her in the burning sun. The flies swarmed. I explained (with the nurses translating) that I was a doctor and I wanted to examine her.

Looking in her eyes, I made the spot diagnosis that anyone could have made: she had bilateral cataracts.

I asked her to stand. She did.

I gave her a walking stick and asked her to walk. She was able to walk.

I explained to the family, "Your Gogo has cataracts covering her eyes. She needs an operation to have them removed. Afterwards, she will be able to see."

The nurse translated.

Gogo—who's face had remained down cast for our whole conversation—lifted her face towards the blinding sun....

And smiled.

In the developing word, blindness often drastically reduces lifespan. Blindness means that people become unable to fend for themselves in already difficult conditions.

Yet cataract blindness is an eminently treatable condition. The surgery is inexpensive and it takes about 12 minutes.

I have stood in the room the day after men and women from Swaziland have had cataract surgery. There will never be words to describe what it is to watch as a group of people who were blind just 24 hours earlier, have their white bandages removed from their eyes and find their sight restored. They start to sing. In four, five part harmonies. Without any prompting. They sing songs of praise. Of gratitude.

 To read more by Dr. Maithri Goonetilleke, visit www.soaringimpulse.blogspot.com.
To help restore sight to the blind, consider supporting the work of CBM at www.cbmi.org.

Driving by the Accident

BY JUSTIN MCROBERTS

Everyone rubbernecks. Everyone. Rubbernecking is one of the great common denominators of all humanity; that and disdain for the New York Yankees. Recently I have been wondering, is it possible that rubbernecking is more than just the manifestation of some deranged fascination with death or the mindless activity of self-centered commuters? Maybe there is something more to it. Maybe there is something deeply "human"—in the best sense of the word—about the way we slow down and stare at tragedy.

Here is what I mean: When we hear stories of firemen running into burning buildings or private citizens trekking to Louisiana to help rebuild homes, our hearts are moved. We call these people "heroes"—and rightfully so. But perhaps in these moments when we catch a glimpse of heroism in our fellow men and women (or even in ourselves), we are not so much transcending our humanity, but fully embracing it. Perhaps our best moments are our most human moments and vice versa: our most human moments are our best moments. Perhaps the times we place ourselves in the face of danger or even death are inspiring for the very reason that we recognize "the best of who we are" in those moments; not some distant shadow of a kind of person we could never be.

I am suggesting that what is *inhuman* is to simply drive by without even slowing down. Similarly, what is inhuman is to hear stories of injustice or tragedy but remain unmoved, unmotivated and unchanged. What is inhuman is when we hear that 5000 young girls are trafficked in the sex-trade every day, yet we choose to believe they are someone else's responsibility—someone else's daughters. What is inhuman is when we learn that that 30,000 people die daily (five million each year) due to preventable, hunger-related causes, but we tell ourselves that they are someone else's children.

Perhaps what is most inhuman is to know of the deep brokenness that defines much of the world we live in, but to stand in judgment of God for not "doing something about it" when all along, we are the ones who have yet to move.

There is something provocatively human in the way we rubberneck to see what tragedies have affected our fellow humans. And something gloriously human in the actions of those who give their own time, treasure, talent and voice to love, heal and advocate for those who have been abandoned by the inhumanity of the masses.

Justin McRoberts is a singer, songwriter and speaker. Central to his work is advocacy on behalf of the poor and oppressed, predominantly through Compassion International. Hear and read more from Justin at www.justinmcroberts.com.

All Children Have Good Cents

BY DAGMAR SEROTA

I love children, and I love Oakland, California. My volunteer work combines both of these passions every day.

Oakland is a town of contrasts. We have hills and flatlands. We have wealthy and poor. Most of what you hear about Oakland—thirty-five percent graduation rates from high school, violent crimes, gangs, drugs, and high asthma rates in children who live near our smoggy port—is true. Oakland is a community that needs help.

Three years ago, I started Good Cents for Oakland, an organization that teaches kids that they can make Oakland a better place. I tell kids that they can be agents of change by learning about the issues affecting our city, voting for a cause to support, and collecting pennies and other coins (hence the name "Good Cents") to go to the nonprofit they've chosen.

Some of the kids I work with live in the hills; their needs are, for the most part, met every day. They have food, clothing, books to read, and a computer at home. I also work with kids in the flatlands who don't always get steady meals, may not have two parents at home worrying about whether their homework is finished, and may not have shelter every night. It's easy to see the differences between these two groups of children, but few people get to see, as I do, what they have *in common*. *All* the kids I work with are hopeful and want to help others, even those children who could rightly choose to help only themselves.

When I first started Good Cents, a friend of mine told me

about a classroom service project that she had spent weeks working on with other parents. At the close of the project, all the parent volunteers, teachers, and children gathered to celebrate their success. At the event, her son raised his hand and asked, "Why did we *do* this?" After all of the work and long hours, her son, who she hoped would learn from the experience of helping others, was completely disengaged!

How different the experience, though, when children are given the opportunity to choose how to help; when they are given a few ideas and options and then asked what *they* would like to do. Whether they are from the hills or the flatlands, when approached in such a way, they usually go beyond our expectations with their involvement and enthusiasm. It's one thing for an adult to say to a kid, "Here's what we're going to do to help our city"; it's an entirely different thing to say, "What do *you* think we should do to help our city?"

On school-wide voting day, when kids get to choose how to help Oakland, the excitement is palpable. The kids cast their ballots for a cause (hopefully the first of many ballots they'll cast in their lives), and they understand the importance of their vote. When all is said and done—a cause has been chosen and their Good Cents put to use—their smiles beam as they see the positive impact they've made on their community.

Letting kids make meaningful decisions about how to help their community is powerful. It's like throwing a rock into a pool and watching the ripple effect. The kids run with it, then the parents and teachers get excited, people in the community get inspired, and an organization that serves our city gets the benefit so that the ripples can continue through their good work.

I love children, and I love Oakland. I especially love what happens when you put the two together.

For more information about Good Cents for Oakland, visit www.goodcentsforoakland.org.

Meant for this Moment

BY GINA GARCIA

I loved all the prep work for The Princess Project: printing and mailing flyers, asking friends and colleagues for dresses and financial gifts, and sorting through the dresses that poured in as donations. Yet, until I finally had the chance to help girls choose a dress, I had no real clue what The Princess Project was truly about.

Girls began lining up at 5:00 in the morning for the big day at The Princess Project where they hoped to find a beautiful dress they couldn't otherwise afford for their prom. Helping the girls sift through racks and racks of various styles, grabbing handfuls to try on at a time; cheering and laughing with the girls when a dress zipped right up; tucking in bra straps, tying, knotting, wrapping, layering, and accessorizing to create the desired "look"—this is what warmed my heart. This is what it was about. But there was more.

In the midst of all the activity, I noticed a girl standing alone, appearing disconnected. I asked her if she had found a dress; her response was that the event was "lame" and she didn't like any of the dresses. But I saw that she kept glancing at the rows of clothes. I thought that perhaps she was embarrassed to try one on in front of anyone else. I glanced at her to judge her size, then walked over to one of the dress racks, grabbed one, and asked her gently, "What do you think of this dress? Do you like the color? I bet it will fit!" She shrugged and looked away. I then told her, "You can take this home and you don't even have to try it on. You don't even have to tell anyone you didn't try it on." Her face lit up and she looked at me and said, "Really? I don't have to try it on?" And I said, "Nope, you can just take it with you. I bet you would look beautiful in this dress." She looked at me and said, "Thank you." This girl would have left without a dress, but I was able to help her find one. I realized all of those years in retail were meant for this moment. From then on, I just started snatching dresses off of the racks and handing them out. I was thinking, "No one leaves without a dress!"

Hundreds of girls walked out of the building that day with a big grin and a beautiful dress. I was lucky to be able to witness and experience their joy; it is something I will never forget.

Gina Garcia has been involved with The Princess Project for three years and has served on the Steering Committee as The Girl Outreach Chair. She is currently a Mentor for Team In Training which supports The Leukemia and Lymphoma society, and will be running her second marathon this October. For more information, please visit www.princessproject.org.

Helping Those Without Speech

BY PATRICIA BROWN

In February of 1963 I turned eight years old. We lived on the second and third floor of an old Victorian House on Bristol Pike in Bensalem, Pennsylvania. I have a picture of me on my birthday (my mom was always snapping pictures). I'm wearing a dress my mom had made for me, a coat she may have sewn as well, and I'm holding my dog Mitsy in my arms, albeit very awkwardly. Mitsy was a quarter my size after all. She was a Cocker Spaniel and I loved her.

The following summer was rough, ending the childhood reflected in this photo. I was the one who found my father after he tried to commit suicide—the first of many traumatic events that turned a fairly normal childhood into a terrifying nightmare with horrific instability. The trauma would affect us all, even poor Mitsy, who "accidentally" fell off our second story balcony and was never the same. She did remain, however, my companion, confidante and comforter for a short while.

Years went by and I was passed from person to person, home to home, changing schools sometimes several times in one year. I seldom felt wanted, even when placed with family and friends. I longed to have my own home and to feel loved. I finally graduated from high school, worked in a piano factory for three years and then attended college where I met my husband. Our marriage resulted in twenty more years of trauma—my husband was controlling, angry and abusive. Knowing it would not be wise to have children with such a man, I longed for a dog. Apparently, this was too much to hope for as well. When I brought up the possibility, he would angrily announce that dogs were dirty and would not be allowed inside.

I eventually left my husband and met someone kind and gentle—someone who loved me enough to give me a puppy. On my 47th birthday, I finally had my dog, a beagle named Charlie. Although Charlie was a challenge at first, I found that having a dog was one of the most wonderful experiences in my life. I quickly realized that animals have their own personalities, likes, dislikes, and emotions. They have ways of communicating their needs if we would only learn to listen. Or maybe it's just me; I seem to have a unique gift for knowing what they need. Due to my history, I still find it hard to trust and open up to people, but I can be myself with dogs and we seem to understand each other.

My life now includes many dogs, as I found my niche in volunteering as a dog-sitter. I especially love taking in homeless dogs while they wait to be adopted. These dogs have usually been mistreated in their past, and they need special patience and care. One of the beagles I fostered seemed to have escaped from a testing laboratory. She would tremble terribly at the vet and freeze up in the presence of anyone wearing a white lab coat. She had many scars on her body that were probably from tests; tests done without anesthesia. I named her Boo because she was so easily startled.

I decided to keep Boo. It took a year to housetrain her and almost as long before she would venture close enough to be petted. Her normal pattern was to surface from under the bed to eat and, if approached, quickly return to her hiding place. But then came the day when she unexpectedly hopped into my lap. It was a moment of indescribable joy for me and a turning point for Boo. Before long she was sleeping in my bed, curling up beside me with Charlie, and I had two warm and furry heaters in my bed!

Knowing how much love a pet can give to a person, it is my hope to unite other homeless pets with people who could use the company. When you reach out to a hurting dog, you can almost see the gratefulness in his eyes, and your life is blessed so much in return.

There are numerous ways to serve pets. Most shelters and veterinarians welcome volunteers, and even your neighbors could probably use help with their pets. You can also serve others *with* pets by visiting a nursing home with a mellow dog, for example, or by learning to train service dogs. Patricia Brown is a retired secretary with a masters in holocaust studies. She is the book review editor for www.giftfromwithin.org, a support site for women with post traumatic stress disorder.

Angels with Four Paws

CHRISTINE GONYEA

"You'll have to pay the $15 fee." The young man sat at his desk in the grey office behind a thick pane of glass, "She's in the infirmary, I'll take you back there." As representative for the NorCal Australian Shepherd Rescue, I had been given the job of transporting a sick rescue dog to the Australian Shepherd Sanctuary. I raised my eyebrows as I got out my wallet and wondered to myself why we should be paying the animal shelter anything at all. After all, I was taking a dog with a tumor off their hands and would surely have vet bills and other expenses as a result. He led me through one dark building full of chain link kennels, then another, and finally into a third building designated as the infirmary.

The dog's kennel mate, a lap-sized mix of some sort, jumped up and walked to the chain link wagging its tail, while our appointed dog, a little Aussie female, sat there, awkwardly, and looked at us over her shoulder. It took some coaxing to lead her out of the chain link enclosure. That was when I noticed blood and a clear fluid on the cement floor and I stopped to run my hands over her and see how serious the tumor appeared to be. What I found was truly appalling.

Her belly was distended towards the floor by a tumor that must have been about the size of a soccer ball. She had the odor of a sick animal and I wondered if the shelter vet had even looked at her. She gamely stood quietly while I looked her over and then eyed the attendant. "Did you not notice this?" I asked him gesturing towards her stomach and the trail on the floor. My expression must have revealed my shock. He replied, "This is the first time I've laid eyes on her. Do you want to leave her?"

"Oh no," I exclaimed. "I'm taking this dog right now!" I felt I had to get her out of that cold concrete place. She needed help and she needed it fast.

We carefully led the dog outside the building and out to the gate where my truck waited. He helped me lower the crate I had brought with its carefully arranged blankets for the comfort of our canine passenger. After securing the crate and seeing that my new friend was as comfortable as possible, I phoned Kim, my director at NorCal Aussie Rescue. "This dog needs to go straight to the vet right now," I told her as I described the Aussie's condition as best I could. She instructed me to take the dog directly to one of her vets who was open on Saturdays and was just off the highway on my route to the Sanctuary. We hit the road. I tried to drive quickly without hitting too many potholes and rough spots. Every one we hit made my stomach clench in sympathy for my silently suffering passenger.

The vet had been notified of our coming, and we were placed in a private exam room with some towels on the floor until we could be seen. I sat on the floor with the dog while we waited. There was always hope, and I stroked her gently and spoke to her quietly. If my petting slowed down or faltered, she would carefully turn and place her head on my knee or arm, looking me right in the eye with her beautiful blue eyes. "What an angel," I thought to myself. She's so quiet and polite even though she must be in terrible pain. Right then in my mind, that became her name—Angel.

The vet came in the room, looked at me, and then at Angel. She bent down to the floor and looked at her carefully. She said, "I'm sorry, she's too far gone; there's nothing we can do at this point." My heart sank. The vet and her assistant brought in the necessary drugs and gave Angel the shot to relax her. As her breathing eased a little, they gave her the final injection. The three of us sat on the floor together and stroked Angel's silky fur. So quietly that I couldn't even pinpoint the exact moment, Angel slipped away and was gone.

I blinked and was surprised to find tears in my eyes. I looked up; both the doctor and the technician had tears in their eyes, too. Their kind words were more felt than heard by me. They were thankful that I had been there for Angel, that she had my attention and love at the end.

I felt dazed. I clipped a little of Angel's silky hair and then left the vet's office. In the truck, my son waited patiently with my own Australian Shepherds. My dogs were excited to see me as they always are, even when I'm only out of their sight for a few minutes. We drove to the nearest dog park where my son and I sat quietly in the sun and watched the dogs running and playing. I thought of Angel and the people in her life. She must have been a darling puppy once. I thought of her getting sicker and sicker and then being abandoned by her owners. I thought of the people in the shelter who probably should have put her out of her misery days before I came to help.

I took out the lock of fur I had clipped from Angel. I let my fingers slowly open and watched the breeze take the hair away strand by strand to blow across the dog park. I looked up and watched my own dogs wrestling with each other before running off across the park and then running back. They live for the here and now, and enjoy every minute of life as it's happening. This is what I learn from my healthy dogs: to relish life.

But I learned something else from Angel. I learned that it's easy to feel good when you've found a warm home for a neglected dog; to feel a sense of pride and accomplishment when everything turns out well. But there is another side of the rescue coin, which I experienced with Angel. I learned that I'm strong enough to face this side of service, too. Sure it tears at my heart and puts a lump in my throat. But I can do this. I can shed tears for the ones that don't make it, and rejoice for the ones that do.

I took a photo of Angel with my cell phone at the vet's office.

I keep it at my desk so she can continue to be an angel to me, gently reminding me of what's important. My sense of pride and accomplishment is not important; nor is it important that things go exactly as planned. What is important is to be there when needed; to serve in the manner that is required—whether painful or pleasant.

Christine Gonyea is a wife, mother and AutoCAD technician who shares her California home with her understanding husband, teenage son, two full-time Australian Shepherds, three cats and the occasional foster Aussie. She divides her spare time between home, Concord High School Band Boosters and Norcal Aussie Rescue. Find out more about NorCal Aussie Rescue and read wonderful bios and stories at www.NorCalAussieRescue.com.

Sacred Conference Calls

BY MICHAEL GINGERICH

Who would think that a conference call could be such sacred ground; a meeting place for energizing spirits and sharing burdens? I am the monitor of two tele-support groups where I've experienced more community and compassion than I've ever witnessed in any physical place. Maybe it's because there is less perceived vulnerability when you are voice-to-voice rather than face-to-face—resulting, ultimately, in more risks taken and greater openness. Maybe it's because there are fewer physical distractions on the phone—resulting in increased concentration on what is being said and heard. Regardless, I leave each call with tremendous awe and immense respect for those who join in. The kinship we share is deep and unbreakable.

My callers all have in one thing in common: cancer. As a director for the Cancer Recovery Foundation, I established two phone support groups. One group is for those who are currently being treated for cancer and for cancer survivors; the other is for caregivers. Each caller is dealing with a threat to life—a threat that takes more than medicine to face and survive. It also takes caring support, a vital spiritual life, a healthy attitude, and the practical disciplines of good nutrition and regular exercise. These things are hard enough for anyone to maintain, but add the stress of a cancer diagnosis to the mix and things get much tougher.

I have come to realize that stress can have devastating effects on one's health and well-being. I have three sons. The youngest, Matthew,

THE SOCIAL CAUSE DIET

was born with severe mental retardation and was later diagnosed with autism. The care and nurture of a child with disabilities takes a heavy toll on any family, a toll that is sometimes hard to measure. As a pastor, I was in demand 24/7, working and tending to my parish over 60 hours a week. The main responsibility of caring for Matthew and our other two sons fell to my wife Kathy. As mothers often do, she neglected her own needs and her health began to deteriorate. In fact, I saw it coming well before her cancer. As her blood pressure climbed and her diabetes grew worse, I took a leave of absence and eventually found a new job that allowed me to be more present at home. Then came Kathy's cancer diagnosis, and more than ever, I made it a priority to help her take care of herself.

Kathy is now a breast cancer survivor. I believe our efforts to reduce her stress and take a whole-person approach to her treatment contributed to her present health. With this very personal experience of being there for my wife through her diagnosis, partial mastectomy and radiation therapy, I now lead the phone support groups, sharing this intense journey with others who are learning to live—and live well—with cancer in their midst.

What do we talk about on these calls? Sometimes we talk about fear—the fear of test results, the fear of the cancer coming back, the fear of pain, the fear of being left alone, the fear of death. Sometimes we talk about anger—at the disease, at the medical profession, at family members, at insensitive friends. Sometimes we talk about regrets—about things left undone, about mistakes that were made, about opportunities not taken. But always... always... no matter how difficult the topics of discussion might be, the calls ultimately energize and strengthen us. They are always affirming and encouraging, with essentially no criticism or judgment. With every conversation and the collective wisdom that comes from it, callers are relieved of their burdens, if only for that hour. But at least for that hour. And as that hour relieves some of the stress, there is healing.

We have had a number of callers who were told they would

only have three months, six months or nine months to live. Yet, they are living significantly longer—sometimes more than a year beyond what they were told. These are the folks who adhere to the Cancer Recovery Foundation principle that an integrated, whole-person approach is the best way to treat cancer. These folks are changing their diets, getting more exercise, seeking the company of affirming people, learning to be positive, and deepening their relationship with God. They are stepping back from "toxic" relationships while diligently working on forgiveness. Basically, they are filtering out things they believe to be of lesser importance and prioritizing those that which bring joy and peace.

One of my callers decided to hike the entirety of a hundred-mile trail. Another sold her business and is currently traveling around the country with her best friend, joining our phone group whenever she can get cell phone reception. One man traveled to Suriname to learn more about healing plants in the Amazon rainforest. Several have gone on weeklong retreats to learn more about the impact that stress, attitudes, perceptions and relationships have on our health and healing. Kathy and I are traveling more often. We've gone to Hawaii and London, even though the trips were expensive. We believe it's too expensive *not* to do these things.

During our tele-sessions, there may be tears, but there is also laughter. Humor is a huge stress-reliever. One man with colon cancer joked that when he first got sick and was scheduled for a colonoscopy, his wife exclaimed, "Well, maybe now we'll find out what that bug is up your ass." Of course she was commenting on his negative attitude—which he no longer has!

Over and over again, I hear how vital these groups are to the participants' survival, well-being and spirits. The cherished connections we make with each other provide a measure of peace to help us through another week. We are all people who know how difficult the journey is. We are people who just want others to listen with compassion and patience.

This is the most important and profound service I offer—compassionate listening. And everyone follows suit with generous listening and sharing. Together we form a place of trust, intimacy and healing; a sacred place that reminds us that we are not—and never need to be—left to face this disease alone.

For more information on Cancer Recovery Foundation, go to www.cancerrecovery.org. New callers are always welcome. If you have questions, please call 800-238-6479.

Fried Turkey and Boiled Crawfish

BY MATTHEW CALKINS

The shotgun style house stands about a city block from the Mississippi River in uptown New Orleans. The street wasn't flooded during Hurricane Katrina but the wind blew old Mr. G's roof to pieces—which is what can happen when you're too poor to pay for termite treatment. The rain did the rest of the damage; by the time Mr. G and his sister, Miss B, got home, there wasn't any way to save the walls. Like so many in the city, they needed to gut and chuck and start to rebuild.

It took two years to find help, because they sure didn't have enough money to go it alone. Forget insurance, and they weren't getting much from the government. But they had friends and they had church. And the time came when they wound up at the top of the list of the Rebuild program of the Episcopal diocese of Louisiana. Every week a different group of volunteers came by and took a turn. When it was our turn, the job was well underway. The walls had been stripped and rewired and reinsulated. New vinyl windows were set in the old frames. Although creaky and crooked, the old reprobate started looking pretty good with its new clothes on, in this case gypsum drywall and a first coat of tape and compound.

We were the ones who dressed it up. No big thing except that none of us had ever done anything like this work. But we came for a reason—to help—and the diocese had a couple of twenty-somethings who showed us what to do. Kiel was the teacher; he'd already worked for six months. Mike was the other one, just a few months in. Talk about positive role models. After this stint of volunteering, Kiel was off to seminary and Mike to the Peace Corps.

The work started slowly Monday—we had just arrived from home state Connecticut, and everyone was getting to know each other and settle in. We came from six different churches, about half from the city, half suburb. We were black, white, Latino, mixed up. It was a fine group. Pretty soon we were all goofing around and making too much noise and waking up late. Aside from a bit of adult yelling, adolescent roughhousing and one broken window (the other one was already broken when we got there!), we managed to get where we needed to go.

The great thing about these short term mission trips is that they are an immersion in an experience that can't help but open your eyes to some things you need to see. The main thing is the people you meet. People whose lives are hard and who need our help. People whose faith in God teaches us what really counts. People who show us Christ in action. New Orleans is full of abandoned houses and people waiting for help. But it is also full of new life and old beautiful homes and a funky sort of jazz, jubilee and we'll-get-through-anything sort of spirit. Times are hard, but they are not hopeless.

By Thursday we were old hands. The place was sheetrocked and taped and about done. It was time to feast. Mr. G had been out back all day, cooking. We gathered around a makeshift table, grabbed some paper plates and waited. The pastor carved up a golden fried turkey while Mr. G finished cooking another one. A huge mess of boiled crawfish smelled incredible. We got a lesson in how to eat them: take off their head and the end of the tail, strip off the shell and it's that morsel of spicy, salty meat that pops into your mouth. We said grace. Mr. G was visibly moved when he thanked us for our work.

We dug in and ate. And it was good.

Rev. Matthew Calkins pastors St. Timothy's Episcopal Church in CT. Read more by Matt at www.sttimschurch.com. Your neighborhood churches may offer similar mission trips.

A Gentle People's Last Hope

BY ERIC P. NICHOLS

Modern geography is a lesson in atrocities. It seems we never know a country exists until we hear of some horror or tragedy coming out of it. Who ever heard of Darfur, or Rwanda or Uganda during "normal" times? Or even going back a few years, did anyone have a clue where Viet Nam was before the war?

The nation of Myanmar has come into the public consciousness of late, but it has been in a state of dire crisis for at least fifty years. It's a long, complicated, sordid history. First, let us set the record straight and mention that no freedom-loving, pro-democracy citizen of that country refers to it by the name Myanmar. Myanmar was a name imposed upon the people by the brutal, illegal military regime, one that routinely uses children as human minesweepers. It is still Burma. It will always be Burma.

In the jungles of Burma, along a 1,500 mile border shared with Thailand, are about 2,000,000 internally displaced persons (IDPs), most of whom are minority ethnic groups who have been burned out of their villages by the ruthless military regime. They have been on the run, hiding in the jungle, living a raw subsistence, for decades. The lucky ones manage to get into one of hundreds of refugee camps on the Thailand side. The rest are doomed to spend their entire lives on the run.

Burma supports a vast army, while the rest of the citizenry is perpetually on the verge of starvation. Within 60 years, Burma has degenerated from the "Emerald of the Orient" to a backwards, paranoid, isolated island of insanity, while all their neighbors are embracing, or at least testing out, progressive, pro-democracy paths. Burma has no external enemies; the massive army exists for one sole purpose: the genocide of their own minority people groups.

The largest of these minorities are the Karen Hill Tribes, a gentle, civilized, gracious nation-within-a-nation. The Karen are of Tibetan descent, but have lived in Burma long enough to have a unique, refined culture of their own. They are the loveliest and most hospitable people you will ever meet.

And they have been targeted for extinction by the Burmese Army, for no other reason than that they are not ethnic Burmans.

Precious few people know about the plight of the Karen, and even fewer are doing anything to help them. However, there is one intrepid, heroic group of people who do put their lives on the line daily to seek out and supply aid to these IDPs deep inside Burma: The Free Burma Rangers.

I have been most privileged to have been associated with the Free Burma Rangers since year 2000. Now, I have to confess, my association has been rather cushy and safe. My trips into the Burma jungle have been short and tentative. The core of the Free Burma Rangers actually *lives* inside Burma. Each one of them has a price on his/her head…simply for showing compassion toward the Karen and other IDPs. These people need our support and encouragement.

One doesn't need to be a Rambo to help these people, though in some cases it's helpful. My first visit to the area was to the refugee camps on the Thailand side. I went with a group of eleven people to visit the orphanages in the camps. The largest of these camps, called Mae La, has more people than the entire town of Fairbanks, where I'm from. It was a staggering, eye-opening experience for someone like me, who'd never been to a third world country. The operator of the orphanage there was a Mother Teresa sort of lady, named Rose Mu. She had horror stories of her own to tell, having spent too many years in a Burmese prison, but she didn't spend a lot of time dwelling on that. She saw her job as giving these orphans as normal a life as possible. I figured that was something I could do for a few hours as well. We spent an afternoon there giving the kids toys we had brought, as well as oranges and other fruits that were rare commodities in the refugee camps. Since we were all tall "Farang" (foreigners), the kids were thrilled when we picked them up so they could touch the ceiling of the orphanage. After lifting 80 kids high enough to touch the ceiling—over and over again—you just about feel like you've gone through Rambo training. But it was the happiest time in my life, as well as for the kids, judging by the gleeful squeals.

It was a wonderful diversion for us and the kids, although we were acutely aware that reality would return soon enough. We left knowing these kids were still orphans. Some of them were missing limbs as a result of contact with land mines. The sheer immensity of the human need was beyond comprehension. But, at least for that afternoon, we felt we were doing something meaningful and necessary. And it didn't hurt a bit…well, other than some aching arms from extensive orphan-lifting.

Upon returning from that trip, spending several weeks visiting refugee camps and getting the "lay of the land," I wrote an article called, "The Ministry of Showing Up." It was a frank admission of utter helplessness we feel when confronted with such staggering needs and the realization that sometimes all you can do is show up and let people know you at least KNOW of their plight. The good news is this: Showing up is usually more than enough. People there keep telling us how important it is. So we keep on doing it.

On my fourth trip to the border, I took my daughter with me; a great reality check for her too. We visited this beleaguered village called Kee Koo Du Kee. Although not a refugee camp, it is an appallingly impoverished area. We brought in some food, blankets, medical supplies and other basics. There was a middle aged lady there, whose name translated means "Golden Ring." We got to know her pretty well. She had seen her husband brutally murdered by the

Burmese army just a couple of years earlier. Golden Ring asked me where my wife was. I explained that she wasn't as adventuresome as I was, and was taking care of our youngest daughter still at home. Golden Ring handed me this beautiful hand woven Karen handbag… probably worth a couple of month's wages. She told me to take it to my wife and tell her she loves her for letting us come. How does one *possibly* respond to that? That handbag, naturally, is a prized possession in our home in Fairbanks.

It isn't always about fixing things; sometimes it's just about caring. Sometimes it's about exposing atrocities. Sometimes that works. And sometimes it doesn't.

I would like to say that, in the case of Burma, international political pressure would be helpful. However, the military regime has again and again proven to be completely immune to public opinion. At this point in time, the IDPs have little relief other than the compassion of the Free Burma Rangers.

I have to admit I feel like a total wimp whenever I meet with one of the Free Burma Rangers and learn of their latest exploits. They are heroes in anyone's book. The least I can do is stand with them financially, let others know about the great work they do, and whenever I can, *show up.*

You can learn more about the Free Burma Rangers at www.freeburmarangers.org.
Eric P. Nichols lives in North Pole, Alaska. He has worked as a broadcast engineer, research engineer, and technical writer and has fit in five trips to the Thailand/Burma border since 2000. He has one published novel, *Plasma Dreams,* and is currently marketing its "prequel," *Steel Stonehenge.*

Street Star

BY BRENDA K. BLAKELY

Walking into the Rock House street ministry in Jackson, Mississippi was an assault to the senses. Carey, a teenager at my church, had invited me to come hear him play guitar in a free concert for street people. All he had given me was an address. I had no idea what to expect from the evening.

The old office building had received a facelift since I had last seen it. Remodeling had changed the front of the building and new carpeting and paint covered up cracks and structural problems, but nothing could hide the odor of the life that had been there.

Mississippi's summer heat exaggerated the musky smell that grew even stronger as we ascended the stairs. I had invited my husband to join me and right then I was glad that I did.

All I could see were dirty people, vividly scarred by all that life on the streets has to offer. The occasional percussion of gunshots punctuated the music. I had no idea what God would show me amid this rubble.

After the initial shock wore off, I began to feel at home. It was a strange feeling. To my chagrin, I realized I wanted to be here. There wasn't a rational reason for this, but my heart longed for something that I couldn't identify and I instinctively knew it was here. This night was the beginning of a new commitment to service in my life.

From that point on, each time the Rock House door opened I was there with my husband, taking an active part in the work to be done. Standing in the crowd one evening, I realized if I was going to be of any real use to these people, I needed to ask God to help me love them.

Loving people is not something that comes to me naturally. With me, God had His work cut out for Him. Yet, I did my part. My commitment remained constant. I went through the motions of caring, feeding and listening to the people who came into the ministry.

One night, anxious to put the sight, smell and sounds behind me after the concert and meal, I dashed for the stairs. But I had to slow down as I approached a coarse, smelly woman blocking the stairway as she hunkered over on the step.

Looking down at her, I first noticed her matted hair. Underneath it was brown; on top there were streaks of blond. Her donated clothes were several sizes too small, although she had made an effort to coordinate them in color.

When I stalled, she began to talk. Not wanting to be rude, I turned toward her to listen. As she began to ramble I suspected she had blocked the stairs as a means to obtain a listener. Her conversation centered mostly on her young years as a child of the streets. I learned her name was Carol, and her struggles of finding a place to rest her head and obtain a decent meal stirred my sympathies. I would never have guessed she was only 25 years old had she not told me.

In her frank conversation several things became apparent. She was street-wise and had learned well the lessons of survival. Here sat a young lady with years of experiences that would have crushed the spirit of the faint-hearted. She was also hungry, yet she hadn't eaten the one sandwich we had given her. She clutched it tightly in her hands.

As we talked, an older man who was her friend wandered across the street. She spotted him coming and quickly explained, "He didn't go to the concert this evening because he wasn't feeling well." From the corner of my eye I could see the old man ambling closer. She continued to share her experiences with me. Quietly and without any pretense or show, she slipped her sandwich into the hands of the old man. Without the slightest hesitation, he began to eat, indicating it had been a while since he had partaken of food.

When she realized I had seen her pass the food to the old man, she commented, "I really wasn't hungry," and went on to share another experience of her time on the streets. With the telling of each experience the sag in her shoulders lessened, somewhat.

My husband, who was one of the other workers, began to come down the stairs. From his vantage point he had noticed the sandwich transaction. He turned and headed back up.

Again he descended toward us. Discreetly, he tucked something into the young woman's hand. She glanced at it and began stuffing it into her mouth in a manner that graphically expressed the urgent need of her body for nourishment. In my mind, I saw a flashback of the sandwich she had passed to the old man and was reminded of her comment, "I wasn't hungry."

Darkness began to fall quickly, closing the curtains on this drama. Carol went back into her world and I into mine. In the theater of life, God had presented this drama to quietly teach me about love, starring an unlikely, yet touching young lady.

These days I look at The Rock House with new eyes. I now cherish the sight, smell and sounds. I thank God, my Father, for intervening in my life and helping me look beneath the rubble to see a jewel.

One day Carol was caught in the senseless violence of the streets, and she no longer dwells in this world. By the grace of God and through the faithfulness of His servants in this street ministry, she had the privilege of meeting Jesus before she was taken from us.

I miss Carol, my Street Star, but it is my prayer that her story lives on.

Brenda Blakely is an educator/writer/counselor. In their fifth decade of life, Brenda and her husband Joel earned M.Ed. degrees and became a traveling team that relishes setting up reading programs and ministries for various populations and cultures. Occasionally serving as adjunct college professors in their hometown, their lives thrive on a steady stream of interesting circumstances, people and opportunities.

Our Boy

BY SHANNON LOWE

Yesterday I met the boy we sponsor through Compassion. All this time we thought his name was Mukanga Dissan, but it turns out that Dissan is actually his first name.

We all met at a well-known Chinese food restaurant (yes, I came to Africa to eat Chinese food), and the Compassion workers brought in the children. Dissan looked a little nervous, until I approached him. He saw the soccer ball I was carrying for him, and his face broke into a smile so big it could light up this hemisphere. He couldn't even bring himself to put down the soccer ball for the first 30 minutes.

We sat down to eat, and his eyes were as wide as saucers. This was not only his first visit to the city, it was his first time to eat at a restaurant. He's nine years old.

We began to go through the backpack full of goodies I brought from home. His eyes nearly came out of his head. He couldn't believe the clothes (they were a perfect fit) and his mouth hung open at the $1 solar-powered calculator. He must have said "thank you" to me a thousand times.

The Compassion worker from his project in the village made the four-hour drive with him, and she served as our interpreter. She and Dissan together told me his story.

He lives in the village, in a mud hut. Both his parents died last year, and the relative he was sent to live with is very sick. So is his six-year-old brother. Because it has rained so much in Uganda the last few months, the front wall of their hut has washed away.

This boy, this precious boy with the golden smile, does not have parents, and he does not even have four walls.

He could not believe the constant flow of food brought out to us (it was served in courses). He devoured everything in front of him, including four egg rolls and two bottles of soda (he was amazed that the waiter brought him a second one).

After lunch, we kicked around the soccer ball in the yard of the restaurant—the boy has a wicked strong kick. I showed him a picture of my children and he asked me when he could meet them.

Parting was terribly hard, especially now that I've seen mud huts in the villages and I know what he's returning to. The interpreter helped me tell him that I love him, and that my family prays for him every night.

He told me that he's praying for us too. Imagine.

I told him that I promised we would continue to sponsor him through Compassion as long as he needs us, until he's an adult. I gave him a long momma hug, which he eagerly returned. I whispered in his ear the blessing I say over my own kids before they get on the bus each morning: May the Lord bless you and keep you, may He make His face to shine upon you, may He be gracious unto you and grant you His peace.

And when he was gone, I hid my face in Sophie's shoulder and wept.

When you sponsor a Compassion child, it is not a "symbolic" sponsorship. Your money is not going into some generic slush fund and doled out to a random group of children. There is only one Dissan, and he is ours. If we didn't sponsor him, he wouldn't have a sponsor unless someone else signed up. If you're a child sponsor, and you want to visit your child in his home country, then they will arrange it.

Because there's only one of you, and there's only one of them.

 Read more stories from Shannon Lowe's blog at www.rocksinmydryer.typepad.com.
To find your own child to sponsor, visit www.compassion.com or www.worldvision.com.

Music of a Stolen Symphony

BY NIPUN MEHTA

It's a late night on the streets of New York. Larger-than-life size billboards come alive with their glitz, trying to make you want things that you don't really need. Up ahead, I notice a homeless man who doesn't have the things he really does need. Ironic.

"Gift size chocolate bar, one dollar, one dollar," he says while showing a Symphony® candy bar to people walking by. He's rejected. "Just one dollar." Rejected again. "Candy bar, candy bar for you," he shows it to a child walking with her mom. The mom jerks her kid away and moves further.

They say that the homeless are used to taking rejections, but seeing the charades ahead of me, I can't help but feel sorry for him. As I stand next to him, shoulder to shoulder, I pause to see if he will try to sell me the candy. He doesn't. I turn to him and ask, "Hey there, buddy. How are you?"

He looks me straight in the eye, as if startled at my directness. Maybe it is because I am ten minutes early for my dinner meeting, but I feel like I am in no rush at all. "How are you doing today?" I repeat my question.

We start talking. A Hispanic guy named "Hecttttauur", with somewhat dirty clothes, many missing teeth and alcohol-smelling breath. Hector tells me his two-minute autobiography of how he used to be happily married and doing theatre until life threw him a few curve balls. Now he's disgruntled, disillusioned and alone on the streets.

In his right hand, Hector is holding a white plastic bag; in his left hand is the bar of chocolate. He's almost forgotten about it, until I pop the question—"So, where did you get the candy bar?" I mean, I'm not trying to put him to shame (because both of us know that he stole it), but I want him to ground himself in the space of truth … even if it was only for that moment.

For the first time, Hector looks down at the ground and says in a lower volume, "I stole it." I don't want to pass a value judgment on his action, so I am silent. After a moment, he continues as if he's talking to a long-lost brother—"But what am I supposed to do? Life is so hard. I can't even survive out here, so I gotta do what I gotta do." His eyes are still looking to the ground and I'm just holding the space of silence.

I pull out my wallet, spontaneously. "Hey buddy, you are selling this for a dollar right?" Now, *he's* silent. "Here's a dollar for your candy bar. But this is what I want you to do with the candy bar: I want you to give it away freely, with an open heart, to someone you don't know." I give him a gold-colored dollar coin that I had received as change from the train ticket booth.

"Just give it?" he replies as if it's a novel concept to him.

"Yeah, give it away. You receive a lot when you give," I say with a heartfelt smile.

Almost as a child, he innocently counters, "But will they punch me if I give it away?"

Huh? It takes a good five seconds to process that question. Who would worry about being punched when giving? I realize that the concept of giving is so foreign to Hector, he doesn't even know what to expect. I can't believe it. I almost have tears in my eyes. It's one thing to be hurting because you don't have basic necessities of life, but what poverty to not know the feeling of selfless giving!

"No, no, Hector. When you give, you don't get hurt. It will expand you. Whoever you give to will be happy and you will be happier because of that," I tell him. By now, I can see that Hector is trusting me. "But you gotta give it away, ok?"

"Ok," he says with a new gleam in his eye.

That bar of chocolate, Hershey's® Symphony, is still in Hector's left hand as I leave. But now it is almost as if he has found the music in his stolen symphony.

 Additional stories of random acts of kindness can be found at www.helpothers.org.

PART THREE

Final Reflections & Resources

*"There is no greater feeling in life
than when you have done something
to make a difference in the world."*

JODY BAGNO

Give of yourself, give as much as you can! And you
can always, always give something, even if it is only
kindness! … Give and you shall receive, much more
than you would have ever thought possible. Give,
give again and again … No one has ever become
poor from giving!"

Anne Frank

How Much Do I Give?

You know you have it in your heart be a great volunteer, but you wonder about the logistics. The personality test and the list of volunteer matching networks in this book will help immensely, but first of all, how do you determine how much of yourself to give?

It would be nice if there was an exact science to the Social Cause Diet, but there isn't. Often people say, "Just do your best." I find this suggestion to be thoroughly unsatisfactory. I do not know what my "best" is! Is it visiting my aging neighbor once a week or once a month? Is it sponsoring one child or two or three? Is it missing a night of sleep to be with a friend in need or saying after an hour, "That's enough; I have to go." Occasionally we will wear ourselves out for the sake of service. That's okay; it doesn't necessarily mean we went too far. It could just mean we were self-sacrificial, and that's a beautiful thing. So how are we supposed to know how much service is healthy and how much is too much?

Try as we may, we can't find any hard and fast rules. We each have to work out for ourselves what we can do and not do and frequently revisit our decisions as the circumstances in our lives change. Here are some ideas that will help as you think it through:

TEN PERCENT FORMULA

One of my friends came up with a formula. He decided to apply the ten percent tithing principle to his time. For years, he had been giving ten percent of his income away, and that was working well, so why not give ten percent of his time, too? His waking day was at least 15 hours long, so he figured he would give 1.5 hours away in service to others. I thought his goal was extremely honorable, and maybe it would work for you. Personally, I'm too sporadic in the way I live my life to do the same.

YES, NO, OR MAYBE

Another approach is to determine if you are a "yes" person, a "no" person, or a "maybe" person. If you are a "yes" person, then you are someone who wants to help everyone and everywhere, often at the expense of your own family or sanity. If this is you, then you need a system of checks and balances. I'm sure, if you're married, your spouse would love to be that for you. If not, check yourself with a few questions before adding more volunteer activities. Ask:

- Am I giving so much that I am getting resentful?

- Am I giving so much that I am neglecting my family or other responsibilities that are clearly mine alone to fill?

- Am I taking on a volunteer task that really doesn't suit my particular strengths and could lead to burnout?

- Am I saying "yes" simply because I don't like saying "no"?

If you answered "yes" to any of these questions, then you need to muster up the courage to say "no" more often. This is so hard, I know. Try to keep in mind that you are not omnipotent or omnipresent. You can't be in more than one place at one time, and, frankly, there may be someone else who would do the job better than you if you decline it. Okay…maybe not, but still, you need to keep the above questions and your priorities in mind. The Social Cause Diet is going to backfire if you aren't able to say "no" when necessary.

Funny how courage is needed to say "no" if you are a "yes" person, but it is needed to say "yes" if you are a "no" person. A "no" person, when asked to do something, thinks—and maybe even says out loud—"Why would I want to do that?!" If you are of this kind, then this book is seriously meant for you! Jabs aside, there is something to admire about such people. When they do say "yes," their commitment is usually a hundred percent solid. When they say "yes," they usually say it for the right reasons. And when they say "no," they are usually trying to protect something—sure, their own self interests, but they are also trying to protect their time with their family or their position at work. If you are in this camp, ask yourself the following questions when you are faced with a volunteer opportunity that you instinctively want to decline:

- Rather than refuse an opportunity in its entirety, is there a part of it I could do?

- What's the worst thing that could happen if I take on this service? (Remember that nothing has to be forever. There will usually be an appropriate time for you to bow out if the job doesn't suit you.)

- Would I have support from my family and from my employer? (You may be worried about losing time with family and at work but ask those in your life what they think. People are usually supportive of service commitments and they may even want to join you.)

- Am I quick to say "no" because I just don't know what to expect or because I expect the worst?

If you tend to expect the worst, find out more information before making assumptions. Knowing that there's always a back door if things don't go well, challenge yourself to do more than you think you can. And be prepared to impress yourself when you do!

Finally, there are the "maybe" folks. Possibly they are non-committal by temperament. Or possibly, they just want to give themselves time to sort things out. If you tend to be indecisive, give yourself a deadline for making a decision, especially if people are waiting to hear from you. Be kind and let people know when they can expect your definitive answer. Jot your decision date down on your calendar so you won't forget. "Maybe" can be a strong or lame response, depending on your follow-up or lack thereof.

A SIMPLER APPROACH

The simplest guideline for determining how much to give is to ask yourself just two questions: "Am I making a difference?" and "Am

I being changed for the better in the process?" Answering the first question is easy. Whether you are contributing to one person or to many, whether you are making phone calls for a fundraiser or dropping off fruit to a shelter, you are making a difference. There are so many needs out there, every bit helps. The second question is harder. If you come back from serving and you are feeling the benefits of the Social Cause Diet, such as an increase in gratitude and appreciation for your loved ones, you are serving well. But, if those benefits disappear within a few days, you need to serve more! Serve regularly so you can keep in shape! If you feel yourself getting selfish and sloppy, step up your service and maintain it until you're on top of things again.

In summary, how much you give is a personal decision. If you are struggling to find the right balance in your life between giving, working, playing, etc., then you are probably moving in the right direction. As you determine the details of the Social Cause Diet for yourself, I wish you courage, a willingness to take risks, and enough service to keep you strong and healthy.

A Calling and a Caution

People often refer to being "called." They feel a pull on their heart and a nagging in their conscience to serve in a specific way, promote a certain cause, or attend to the needs of a particular population. Their calling may be reinforced by a significant dream or a number of coincidences. For services that take you away from your family and home, some manner of calling is critical. You don't want to end up in Liberia and realize you made a mistake. For services that don't take much time or commitment, you don't need an earth-shaking sign. Just go ahead—sign up and check it out.

My great-grandfather's story is a fine example of being called. So is my husband's. The former involved a vision; the latter, a tuna fish sandwich.

When my great-grandfather, Hugh Taylor, announced to his parents that he thought God was calling him to overseas missionary work, his parents revealed that they already knew about it. They both had received that insight when their son was a little boy, although they had never mentioned it to him—that was God's job. As far as I know, there was no precedent of missionary work in the family. And it was a good thing that the calling was so clear, for although Hugh Taylor loved the people of Siam, his 46 years there were extremely challenging and demanded long separations from his family.

When my husband Scott was called, he was minding his own business eating a tuna fish sandwich. All of a sudden, God sent him a clear message to "Volunteer for Young Life." Scott says that he wasn't thinking at all about this ministry for teenagers. The message was so unexpected, so random, and so clear, he couldn't ignore it. He phoned the organization that week and ended up being a volunteer Young Life Leader for seven years.[1]

A word of caution about callings: sometimes we are called to do a service that doesn't come naturally. All sorts of signs and indicators may be telling us that we should take on a particular responsibility, but our minds are saying, "No way!" If this happens to you, it is likely that the service in question will be the grounds for a growing experience that will shape you into a more mature individual. If you sense this may be the case, don't fight it. Give the task your best effort, and you will come out better for it. There is also the chance that you will happily discover that the service did fit you after all—or even that its requirements changed to accommodate your interests.

When I signed up for my second Mission to Mexico trip, there was no one to fill the role of Housekeeping Captain. Week after week, the captains of the other teams would get up and talk about what was ahead. Then they would briefly announce that someone was still needed to lead the Housekeeping Team. Now, let it be known that I do not like housekeeping. I don't care for it on the home front, much less on a ranch in Mexico. But I sensed that the role was supposed to be filled by me. So I volunteered, and to my surprise, I oddly became excited about my new job.

The biggest surprise came while I was in Mexico. Rather than being assigned the task of cleaning toilets, my team was given the challenge of climbing up the mountain to fix the ranch's sign. This sign was the area's version of the famous Hollywood sign. Made of painted white rocks and visible from a far distance, it greeted hundreds of volunteers who were housed at the ranch each year. Our job was to rearrange the rocks and repaint them. What a custom fit for me! I love the outdoors and am always in want of exercise and adventure. People praised me for hiking up the steep hill like a mountain goat, not knowing that I was thrilled inside. A few times I nearly tumbled down the hill with heavy rocks in my arms, but the weather and the view of the countryside before us was glorious. I felt affirmed and rewarded for doing what I thought I was called to do.

A note for those readers still in school, wondering which classes to take or what careers to pursue: with or without a calling, your job is to discover and develop your strengths, interests and talents. In light of this book and your conscience, you may wonder if one skill is worthier than the next. I don't think so. Yes, there is a huge global demand for teachers and medical experts, but you'd be surprised how various occupations can kick into play when given the opportunity. Investigators and lawyers are needed to fight for justice in every corner of our world.[2] Engineers are in more demand than ever due to the growing interest in sustainable systems.[3] Entrepreneurs, managers, accountants, and entertainers all have opportunities for altruism. My friend Charlie used to be a traveling clown, of all things. Twenty years later, he still keeps his juggling and unicycle skills honed so he can entertain underprivileged kids.

When I was in high school, I decided to pursue a career in graphic design. I wondered if such a profession had any worth on a global scale. I couldn't envision it being very important in the grand scheme of things, but I was confident I was gifted in this area and that I should pursue it. Now, years later, I can't tell you how many nonprofits I have helped with my design business (not to mention start-ups, friends and family members!).

At one point, though, I decided that I had done enough and would no longer give away free design work—or so I thought. That week a wonderful, well-loved man in my community died. I was grieving but had no way to share it because I wasn't close to the family. Then someone called and asked if I would be so kind as to design the program for the man's memorial service. Well, of course I would! I tearfully designed the best program I could to honor him, humbled and thankful for a skill that could be of use.

No matter what interests you pursue or what calling you may have, learn your lessons well and put your heart into them. They will come in handy, professionally and philanthropically.

1. For information on Young Life, visit www.younglife.org.
2. Investigators and lawyers, read about the amazing International Justice Mission at www.ijm.org.
3. Engineers may want to look into Engineers Without Borders: www.ewb-usa.org.

Honor and shame from no condition rise;
Act well your part, there all the honour lies.

ALEXANDER POPE

It is more shameful to distrust our friends
than to be deceived by them.

FRANCOIS DE LA ROCHEFOUCAULD

When Service Goes Awry

When I was in high school, I was introduced to the idea of being a pen pal to a prisoner through Prison Fellowship International. I thought it would be easy enough to write to a prisoner now and then, so I called the organization and asked for a connection. They matched me up with an elderly man who happened to share my Christian faith. A safe match, so they thought. Clyde and I wrote to each other for a few years. I visited him at prison occasionally. Then, out of the blue, Clyde sent me a letter that revealed he had fallen in love with me. Prison Fellowship had hoped he was too old for that, but not so. I wished Clyde well but told him I would no longer be writing.

Six years later, I was living in Chelsea in Manhattan. My side of the street was lined with decent apartments, but the other side was filled with rows of SROs, or Single Room Occupancies. A single room contained everything: a toilet protruding from the wall, a twin bed, and a tiny sink. Charlie was an old man who lived in one of these SROs. I would often see him sitting on the ledge of his narrow window. Not having learned my lesson from Clyde, I befriended Charlie. At least once a week for over a year, I would help him get a little exercise by slowly walking around the block with him. He shuffled around on flat, flimsy shoes. I sometimes guided his arm to help him with a curb. My mom was suspicious of Charlie but I insisted he was a poor old man needing company. Then one day, Charlie landed a big, wet kiss on me! I can still feel his scruffy, pudgy face on my cheek. To be clear, this was not merely a friendly kiss, but an attempt to be romantic. Thereby another round of service ended.

Why do I reflect upon these failures? Because I don't really consider them as such. They didn't end well, but they were certainly worthwhile for a time. Besides, I was doing what I believed was right.

Although I should be sensitive to the vulnerabilities of those around me, I cannot control how those on the receiving end interpret my efforts. Something I *can* do, obviously, is consider a different line of service in the future—maybe something to do with innocent babies—but there's no reason to feel awful for befriending these two men or to write off service altogether.

Another example is something that happened to my college friend, Craig. One evening while Craig was walking to his apartment, a homeless person caught his attention. Within thirty minutes of talking, Craig began to care for the guy and invited him to sleep on his couch for the night. In the morning, the homeless person was gone—along with Craig's wallet. The wallet had been on the table beside Craig's bed, so the theft was especially violating. When Craig told me the story the next day, he was mad (and rightly so), but he was also ashamed. He felt stupid for being taken advantage of. I did my best to say, "No! The homeless person's bad behavior isn't your fault! You did a good thing. You offered a room and your trust to a person who was down and out. The shame does not belong on you."

When we offer others a gift of any sort, it is up to the receiver of the gift to use it well or not. In service, we need to be careful not to blame ourselves for things we cannot help—although it is wise to keep a watch on our wallets!

I would be remiss if I didn't acknowledge that my examples are perhaps trivial and almost sweet. What about those tragic reports of relief workers who are seriously injured or of missionaries who are slaughtered? The movie *End of the Spear* chronicles the story of a family whose father is slain while trying to bring peace to an Amazon tribe that was killing itself off. But the story doesn't end there. In fact, nothing really ends when we think it does. None of us can predict the future or see things in light of eternity, so none of us is in a position to determine when a mission has truly failed. There are countless stories of the phoenix rising from the ashes, hope surviving in unlikely places, and people being affected long after the volunteers pack it up and go home.

Unfortunately, however, there are occasional attempts at service that are misguided, resulting in damage to a person or culture. No individual is perfect—not a single one of us can claim to have perfect motivations or exemplary behavior all of the time. Therefore, no organization that is made up of individuals is perfect (especially if the organization is largely composed of volunteers who come and go). We need to accept imperfection as a condition of existence. If we hold back from serving because things aren't just right, a lot of opportunities will be missed.

This is not to say you shouldn't do your homework and look for an organization with a stellar track record. You can read reviews and rankings of volunteer programs from other volunteers on VolunteerMatch.org. In addition, take some time preparing yourself for your designated service. It's a dreadful thing to discover that you contributed to a mishap. If you ever find that you are part a problem, pull back, get advice and maybe even pick a different service. There are so many to choose from!

In summary, when serving, there are no guarantees that things will work out exactly as anticipated. Giving of ourselves does involve risk and the spirit of adventure. The unpredictability is part of the excitement. Keep your eyes open so you notice the pleasant surprises that come your way, and keep your wits about you when unpleasant ones arise. The Social Cause Diet requires flexibility. If you have a good measure of it, great! If not, proceed with caution so you will be gently stretched and loosened up. The flexibility you gain from being involved in an experience that cannot be perfectly controlled or orchestrated will enhance all areas of your life.

The pessimist sees difficulty in every opportunity.
The optimist sees the opportunity in every difficulty.

WINSTON CHURCHILL

The Whole Process

On my first Mission to Mexico trip, it seemed to me that our team spent as much time playing around as we did serving. We spent half the day doing day camp or construction and the other half talking about it or having fun amongst ourselves. I thought this was imbalanced; I signed up to *serve*, not to have a retreat with my friends! But after a while, I saw that the time we had together resulted in a large part of the satisfaction. In fact, one of the prime reasons for serving within an established organization is for the enjoyment and wisdom found by interacting with colleagues.

Unless you want to restrict your service to the simplest of activities such as taking old clothes to the local GoodWill, be aware that your service will involve more than just serving. It will include preparation, getting to know your comrades, and debriefing—all important parts of the process. The specifics, determined by the type of service and organization, are too varied to articulate here, but basically, your acts of service will very likely take more time and energy than you expected. But isn't that the case with anything worthwhile? Who of us really understands what will be required of us when we decide, for example, to have kids? If we had known, we might not have had them! But fortunately, we take one step at a time and find out that it's okay; we can do it; it's worth it.

The whole process also includes bumps along the way. Especially when you volunteer abroad or with a large group of people, there tends to be a lot of inefficiencies and hurry-up-and-wait scenarios. If you are a highly efficient person, this may be the hardest part! It's understandable: you're giving up your afternoon or day or week, and then another volunteer who doesn't quite "get it" is late and holds up the whole operation. Or you're driving in a caravan and all the cars have to file into yet another gas station because someone drank too much soda and needs a pit stop. Or you end up without enough bread for the day camp because someone messed up the math. How does a competent person go with the flow of such incompetence?

I'm still working on this one myself (can you tell?), but I have come up with one strategy: observe and learn from your seasoned leaders. When you volunteer, hopefully you will have leaders who are calm and flexible when faced with disorder and disappointment. If they are keeping their cool, maintaining compassion, and coming up with solutions, you are lucky to have such examples. Get your eyes off the problems and watch them. Model your own actions and attitudes after them. It's a far better option than fussing and wasting possible opportunities to shine as you step in to help.

When a significant round of service is over, it's time to debrief. I recommend a three-part debriefing plan that consists of journaling, dialoguing and detoxing.

JOURNALING is a powerful reflection method that all of us can easily do with a pen and a notebook. Some prefer a laptop, but most find scribbling on paper to be more intimate. And do be intimate—don't just write about the weather. I'll never forget the dismayed look on my husband's face while he was reading his deceased grandmother's diaries. He was sitting in her beautiful old rocker, surrounded by what he thought would be a window into her soul. He anticipated gleaning wisdom, as well as ancestral details, from the dozen well-worn handwritten books. But they were all about what she ate that day and whether or not it rained!

Effective journaling, on the other hand, is when you write to help clarify what is churning in your mind. Often, things that you don't even know are there come out and take shape as you formulate sentences on paper. Before you know it, you have a map of your thoughts: a map that shows you where you've been and maybe where you should go next. In addition to the insight that comes from the actual discipline of journaling (and it is a *discipline*—don't give up before the good stuff comes), the actual writing process of engaging an additional part of the brain that might otherwise be passive reinforces your thoughts and memories.

Journaling helps you dwell on your volunteering experience long enough to get the most out of it. Even if you don't like writing, I encourage you to jot down a few things you want to remember or improve upon the next time you volunteer.

DIALOGUING is the community part of debriefing. Hopefully your leader will schedule a time to debrief together as a group. This is when you share your highs so everyone can be encouraged. It's also a time to ask questions whose answers may benefit the team. Lastly, you may want to *sensitively* share where there may be room for improvement. But be careful—people have worked hard; they may be drained and in need of praise, not criticism. And, clearly, if you have constructive criticism for individuals, rather than for the entire group, offer that up *privately*.

If your group does not pull together for an official debriefing session, hang out with a few fellow volunteers for a while. Maybe you have something to talk about; maybe they have something to unload on you. Either way, check in with others before moving on. Like journaling, this may be something you don't think you need to do, but you'll be surprised with the benefits if you slow down and take the time for it.

DETOXING is my catchall word for doing whatever is healthy and appealing for you to do to clear your mind and refresh your body after volunteering. If you've been in a dirty campground all week, you might want to indulge in a facial. If you've been confined to a clinic, you might need a walk by yourself in the country. If your service mandated a diet of fried food, you might want to go to an organic market and load up on the freshest veggies and fruits you can find. Whatever you come up with, make the most of it. Relish it. Let it nourish your soul. It's part of the process, part of the Social Cause Diet.

Serving with Your Personality Type

BY JODY BAGNO

There is no greater feeling in life then when you have done something to make a difference in the world. It is what real legacies are made of. Giving back is how we make our own unique mark in the world that can many times outlast our own lives. But unless you have felt called to a particular service, it can be hard to know where to begin.

As a personality specialist, I have designed a simple assessment to help you uncover your natural strengths. When we live and work out of our strengths, the reward is a sort of flow and energy to everything we do. In jazz, we call this vibe. In sports, we call it momentum. In love, we call it passion. By taking this test, your results will reveal to you some good places to start until you find that special niche of service that brings out the best in you.

People often ask if core personalities can be changed over time. The answer is no. Our core emotional needs are based on our God-given type. We can develop positive attributes of all personality types, but it is exhausting to try to continually wear one that isn't ours. On the other hand, when we leverage our natural strengths, we become more energized and engaged in whatever we are doing.

Sometimes people unknowingly try to be something they are not because they have the idea that one personality type is better than another, which, of course, is absurd. While you are taking the following test, challenge any assumptions you may have. The world desperately needs what each type has to offer. Our job is to discover, honor, and nourish our particular traits and find opportunities for them to flourish. The intersection of our natural strengths with worthwhile activities is what provides true richness in our lives.

THE SOCIAL CAUSE DIET
PERSONALITY TEST

Read the four statements in each section. Circle the number of the statement that most sounds like you. If two equally apply and you cannot settle on one, you may mark two. (Sometimes people have two primary personality types.) Remember, there are no right or wrong answers...only answers that you feel describe you best.

When you are finished, add up how many you have of each number; then read the personality description that corresponds with your dominant number.

---

1 I can take almost any experience and turn it into a story

2 I prefer stories that have a point and get to that point quickly

3 I appreciate the finer details of any story so that it is accurate

4 I enjoy listening to stories about people

---

1 My priority in most tasks is to make sure we are having fun

2 My priority in most tasks is to get the job done now

3 My priority in most tasks is to complete them correctly the first time

4 When accomplishing tasks, I work better alongside people

---

1 I like lots of friends but have a tendency to not be good at keeping in touch

2 I prefer having only a few close, loyal friends

3 My friendships run deep and are long-term

4 In most of my relationships, I am the loyal, supportive friend and companion

---

1   I wish I were more organized; it is something I have to work at

2   I organize enough to effectively accomplish what is most important

3   I think in steps and enjoy efficient organization

4   I am good at organizing, especially when it helps other people be more successful

1   My energy level increases when I'm around people I enjoy

2   Interacting with other people drains me unless we are being productive

3   I need to decompress and have alone time to re-energize after being with people

4   I need to be with people and do not enjoy too much time alone

1   One of my weaknesses is that I talk too much

2   One of my weaknesses is that sometimes I say things too harshly

3   One of my weaknesses is that I get stuck in an analyzing and planning mode

4   One of my weaknesses is that I have a hard time confronting people when they hurt or offend me

1   I make decisions based on what everyone will enjoy

2   I make decisions quickly and usually make the right decision

3   I take my time to thoughtfully choose the perfect decision

4   Do I have to make a decision?

1   I like brightly colored clothing

2   I prefer to wear power colors like black, red or strong blues

3   I prefer well-tailored clothes

4   My clothing choices are based primarily on comfort

1   My desk has several mementos from happy occasions

2   My desk is set up to be as efficient as possible

3   My desk is either perfectly organized or it remains messy until I can organize it perfectly

4   My desk has items that remind me of important special relationships

---

1   I need approval, affection and attention

2   I need to be in control and not have my time wasted

3   I have very high standards of excellence in all that I do

4   I need peace, respect, and harmony in my relationships

Total how many you have of each number and then read about the personality type that corresponds to your dominant number. Often people are a blend of two types.

TOTALS			
1	**2**	**3**	**4**

1 = Expressive

2 = Driver

3 = Analytical

4 = Amiable

EXPRESSIVE

As an expressive, you enjoy interacting with people. You are naturally positive and enthusiastic. You most likely have a funny sense of humor. You have a gift for inspiring people. You also have the ability to make almost any task fun for everyone involved. Because you are wired to connect well with others, volunteering for any service through which you have lots of contact with people is best, whether it's with a team of workers or with the people you are serving. You are a good person to put out on the frontlines. You are a wonderful greeter and you help lift everyone's spirits. Be careful not to commit to laborious tasks that you won't finish; you don't want to be seen as flakey. Also try to remember to share the spotlight and not hog *all* the attention. Managing money will usually not be your thing; it is an important task to let others handle. You need to be *with people* because connecting with them is where you shine!

DRIVER

"Bottom-line" is one of your favorite terms. Your natural strength is in getting the job done. You enjoy being in charge because you most likely have the best ideas on how to achieve the goal. You can lead people in powerful ways and would be effective heading up a team to accomplish almost any task. A word of warning: be careful with the emotions of others. Sometimes in pursuit of your goal, you can be too direct and abrasive for some of the other personality types. If you can slow yourself down a little so you don't run over anyone you feel is "in your way," you will be pleasantly surprised at how people will follow your lead. In regards to service, you are best at finding a need and filling it. Since you will be a good worker for just about any cause you believe is important, ask yourself: *What do I think needs to be done to make the world a better place? What injustice makes me angry? Who needs my help and guidance?* Your answers will lead to service opportunities about which you will be passionate.

ANALYTICAL

Your ability to make plans and catch important details is the value you can add to the world of service. You work at a little slower pace in order to think through concepts and ideas and accomplish tasks correctly the first time. You prefer to process a great deal of information so that you arrive at the perfect decision. Because of your high standards, anything you deliver is done with excellence. Your connections with people are not taken lightly because you feel emotions deeply. You are most likely good with numbers, details, and money. You offer wisdom and deep reflection when it comes to making plans. You are comfortable working behind the scenes, making sure there are ready-made solutions for potential problems that may arise. You play a key role in the formation of any organization. Be careful when working nonstop with people, as you will have a tendency to feel their pain deeply and may be easily drained by too much social interaction. Also, watch how much you slow down any process with analysis. Sometimes analysis-paralysis can destroy another person's passion and momentum. Try to stay focused on the end result to achieve it in a timely manner, and you will be rewarded for your important contributions.

AMIABLE

As an Amiable, you are a naturally loving person and wonderful listener. You connect with people easily and genuinely encourage others. You are a consistent, loyal friend to anyone with whom you develop a relationship. Although you may feel shy when first entering a situation or group, you would rather work alongside people than lead the charge. You are a mediator and peacemaker, bringing calm in the face of trials and peace to turbulent relationships. Because you prefer to sit back and observe others, you have the ability to find ironic humor in everyday situations. You can excel in administrative tasks, provided there is a routine nature to them. You are a wonderful support person to whomever is in charge. Whatever you choose to do, make sure you are working *with people.* A virtual service project will not fulfill you. Be careful not to let the Drivers run over you, because you will only take that for a short while before you have a meltdown. Make an effort to speak up for your ideas and for what you think people need in any given situation. Your personality type is a blessing to the people around you, so be confident in yourself and your service abilities.

This personality test is not to be reproduced without the permission of Jody Bagno, speaker and coach for "Building Vibe in Your Organization." Visit www.JazzBC.com. The personality titles used in this test are from *Personal Styles and Effective Performance* by David W. Merrill and Roger H. Reid. This book is a wonderful read for a more in-depth study of the social personality types.

Matching Services

O riginally, years ago when this book was conceived, it was going to be a huge manual where people could cross-reference their personality type with their available time with their particular interests and so on. But such a mammoth project no longer seems necessary, thanks to today's savvy technology and a growing number of online resources. If you go to www.volunteermatch.org, for example, you can enter the location in which you desire to serve and then choose from a long list of serving categories. I put in "Marin County" for a location and "outdoor" for a keyword and then received a list of exciting options: volunteering at a therapeutic horse farm, being a docent at a lighthouse, and cleaning trails for Muir Woods. Then for a completely different kind of search, I put in "Charlotte, NC" and "creative" and came up with interesting opportunities that include scrapbooking with nursing home residents and working in a funky coffee house that supports Habitat for Humanity.

The following is a partial list of awesome networks that match volunteers to projects. Note that there's no place on these sites for you to enter in the amount of time you are willing to give. You will have to look into the individual services that appeal to you and see what they offer. Some organizations would like you to commit on a weekly basis; others would be happy to see you once a month; and others want you on-call for a time of crisis. Some offer once-in-a-lifetime service adventures to far-away places like Costa Rica to help save the sea turtles.

As you consider your choices, remember your personality type. If you're a people-person, don't take a job stuffing envelopes! If you prefer long-term relationships rather than making new friends each time you serve, look for an organization that nurtures a core of volunteers. If you are a "Driver," look for opportunities that would allow for leadership, such as leading inner city youth on a bike tour or heading up a fundraiser. An Analytical will naturally spend more time on this process: analyzing his or her interests and strengths, comparing causes, looking into the details of an organization, and considering how all might align for a satisfying service. Whether or not you are that thorough, bookmark a few of these web sites so you can stay up-to-date on opportunities. Another option is to google your local volunteer center (most cities have them) and let them know of your interest. They will be happy to be of assistance.

However you go about it, just don't put it off too long. Volunteering should not be reserved for senior citizens and the independently wealthy. There's a wonderful Hebrew word for the concept that giving back is an obligation everyone shares: tzedakah [tsuh-dah-**kah**]. Giving tzedakah is considered an important part of spiritual life. Everyone is expected to participate in tzedakah, even those who are needy themselves. With today's resources, there's really no excuse for not getting involved. Enjoy the search—and serving!

Partial List of Volunteer Matching Networks

The Corporation for National & Community Service

The nation's largest grantmaker supporting service and volunteering. Through their Senior Corps, AmeriCorps, and Learn and Serve America programs, they provide opportunities for Americans of all ages to meet community needs. They have a wealth of free online resources on their site. ☛ www.nationalservice.gov

Charity Navigator

Charity Navigator is not exactly a matching service, but they provide helpful information on thousands of charities. Their mission is to help people make intelligent giving decisions by evaluating the financial health of nonprofits. By so doing, they aim to advance a more efficient and responsive philanthropic marketplace. ☛ www.charitynavigator.org

Global Citizens Network

This organization sends short-term teams of volunteers to communities in other cultures where participants cooperate with local grassroots organizations to meet global needs. ☛ www.globalcitizens.org

GLOBE AWARE
Sometimes called a "mini peace corps," Globe Aware offers short-term volunteer vacations that focus on cultural awareness and sustainability. All program costs, including the cost of airfare, are tax-deductible. ☛ www.globeaware.org

IDEALIST
Idealist is an interactive site where people and organizations can exchange resources and ideas, locate opportunities and supporters, and take steps toward building a world where all people can lead free and dignified lives. ☛ www.idealist.org

KING DAY
In honor of Martin Luther King, Jr., Congress designated the King Holiday as a national day of volunteer service. Instead of a day off from work or school, Americans are encouraged to celebrate Dr. King's legacy with citizen action. Visit the "MLK" site for numerous projects and resources. ☛ www.mlkday.gov

POINTS OF LIGHT & HANDS ON NETWORK
A national nonprofit whose core mission is to inspire, equip, and mobilize people to take action that changes the world. Their national network connects millions of volunteers to volunteer centers around the country. ☛ www.pointsoflight.org

VOLUNTEERMATCH
VolunteerMatch is dedicated to helping everyone find a great place to volunteer. The popular site welcomes millions of visitors a year and has become the preferred internet recruiting tool for more than 60,000 nonprofits. VolunteerMatch also offers reviews of volunteer programs by other volunteers. ☛ www.volunteermatch.org

VOLUNTEER ADVENTURES
Volunteer Adventures promotes volunteer opportunities that improve the lives of others and the environment in which we live, seeking to connect worthy local projects with volunteers around the world. ☛ www.volunteeradventures.com

THE VOLUNTEER FAMILY
The Volunteer Family connects families with organizations who welcome family volunteers. They also work with a family's unique situation and interests to create individually tailored volunteer experiences. ☛ www.thevolunteerfamily.org

WORLD VOLUNTEER WEB
World Volunteer Web is part of the United Nations Volunteers (UNV) program and serves as a global clearinghouse for information on volunteerism. Click around and discover a fascinating list of organizations offering volunteer opportunities. ☛ www.worldvolunteerweb.org

Organizations

A Greater Gift, 121

AHEAD Ministries, 85-86

Alpha Pregnancy
Resource Center, 85-86

American Red Cross, 58

Aqua Viva, 146

Avon Walk for Breast Cancer, 69-72

Before Their Time, 81-84

Better World Shopper, 121

The Breast Cancer Fund, 98

Buy Shoes. Save Lives., 68

Cancer Recovery
Foundation, 193, 195-196

CharityFocus, 93

The Children's Nature
Institute, 161-162

Christian Blind Mission, 178

Compassion, 55-56, 207-208

Corazon de Vida, 146

Divine Chocolate, 121

Engineers Without Borders, 221

Free Burma Rangers, 200-202

FreeRice, 80

Gift From Within, 187

Good Cents for Oakland, 181-182

Grounds for Change, 121

Habitat for Humanity, 58

HelpOthers, 93, 211

Human Rights Watch, 140

The Hunger Site, 80

International Justice Mission, 221

The Invisible Children, 141

Kids Helping Kids, 99-101

Moment by Moment, 155-156

NorCal Aussie Rescue, 189-192

Peace Corps, 157, 159

The Prison University Project, 117

The Princess Project, 63-65, 183-184

Public Domain Foundation, 87-89

Rancho De Sus Ninos, 143-146

Relight NY, 147-148

Sacred Bite, 129

SonRise Equestrian
Foundation, 59-61

SweatShop Watch, 121

Teach for America, 139

Ten Thousand Villages, 121

Threshold Choir, 173-174

TradeAsOne, 121

Tri-Valley Haven, 169, 172

World Vision International, 208

Young Life International, 221

*For volunteer matching networks,
see pages 240-241*

Contributors

Bagno, Jody, 231, 232

Batliwalla, Shyla, 139

Bermas, Michelle, 69

Blakely, Brenda K., 203

Blomquist, Sean, 85

Brophy, Jessica, 133

Brown, Patricia, 185

Calkins, Matthew, 197

Costello, Patricia, 163

Ernest, Beth, 103

Escorico, Carolyn, 59

Fishel, Elizabeth, 73

Fisher, Cody, 67

Garcia, Gina, 183

Gingerich, Michael, 193

Gonyea, Christine, 189

Goonetilleke, Maithri, 79, 177

Groves, Shaun, 55

Hairston, Avery, 147

Hayes, Bill, 131

Henrich, Karen, 155

Huckabee, Janet, 57

Kay, Sandra, 169

Lowe, Shannon, 207

Malcomb, Chris, 109

Marquez, Colleen, D.C., 153

Maxwell, Nikki, 157

McLaughlin, Triston, 63

McRoberts, Justin, 179

Mehta, Nipun, 91, 209

Munger, Kate, 173

Nichols, Eric P., 199

Nilson, Larry, 149

Ota, Lisa, 127

Page, Laura, 99

Pauley, Kellie, 175

Reinhardt Reiss, Joan, 95

Sbrana, Michele, 119

Serota, Dagmar, 181

Schaefer, Elizabeth Maynard, 165

Simons, Bette, 161

Steinberg, Jes, 143

Stookey Sunde, Elizabeth, 87

Turner, Lynn, 123

Whitman, Michael, 81

Gail Perry Johnston founded Cupola Press to republish quote books *A Rumor of Angels* for a time of loss and *The Wish & The Wonder* for pregnancy and birth, and to bring to light a concept she had been formulating for years—*The Social Cause Diet*. She welcomes your story of satisfying service for Volume II. Submit through www.socialcausediet.com.

Cupola
PRESS®

LIGHT READING FOR INTENTIONAL LIVING.

www.cupolapress.com

Printed in the United States
203994BV00001B/109-315/P